Kerry Ann Jacobs and Edward Lee Jacobs

Near Misses

Copyright @2022 by (Kerry Ann Jacobs & Edward Lee Jacobs)

All rights reserved. No part of this book may be reproduced in any form or by any electronic or mechanical means, including information storage and retrieval systems, without permission in writing from the publisher, except by reviewers, who may quote brief passages in a review.

This publication contains the opinions and ideas of its author. It is intended to provide helpful and informative material on the subjects addressed in the publication. The author and publisher specifically disclaim all responsibility for any liability, loss or risk, personal or otherwise, which is incurred as a consequence, directly or indirectly, of the use and application of any of the contents of this book.

WORKBOOK PRESS LLC
187 E Warm Springs Rd,
Suite B285, Las Vegas, NV 89119, USA

Website:	https://workbookpress.com/
Hotline:	1-888-818-4856
Email:	admin@workbookpress.com

Ordering Information:
Quantity sales. Special discounts are available on quantity purchases by corporations, associations, and others. For details, contact the publisher at the address above.

Library of Congress Control Number:
ISBN-13: 000-0-00000-000-0 (Paperback Version)
000-0-00000-000-0 (Digital Version)

REV. DATE: 07/20/2022

NEAR MISSES

Defying death does not guarantee serenity!

By:

Kerry Ann Jacobs

Edward Lee Jacobs

Foreword

A war hero. A man with American values and loyalty to family. A good man. An honest man. What happens to these men who save America? Are they valued all their lives? Do they all marry and live happily ever after? Everyone has problems they have to solve, sad times they have to endure! The lucky ones are those who have love and support from their family and friends all their lives and die with integrity and peace with loved ones around them.

This is a story of a young man from Arkansas, who like many young men, joined the service and fought for his country. Jake and many more like him saved America during World War II. But, what happened after the war is what makes Jake the man he was. How many men and women actually keep their heads up high and live their lives being a positive example to others? A life is always about choices, but even people who make honest, rational, and unselfish choices do not always have the happiness they deserve. Every American military veteran should be able to have happiness or at least, peace; but alas, Jake had neither, but he persevered. Throughout his life Jake repeatedly defied death, but yet he lived by his philosophy, "Use your past as a lesson, live today, be positive about tomorrow and always be an example to others through your actions and your words." If we had more Jakes in the world, we would all be a lot happier and peaceful.

PRELUDE

December 1943

Jake never liked to jump off high things; not diving boards, not cliffs and certainly not out of a plane. That was the reason he decided not to eject when his dive bomber malfunctioned. The choice to Jake was simple; stay with the plane and take his chances on crashing. As his dive bomber lost altitude it came closer to the inevitable crash, he braced himself and tried to dismiss the memories racing through his mind. After all, isn't that what happens when you are experiencing a near death episode? The emotional pain and regret of his girlfriend in Arkansas who he left behind six years earlier kept flashing through his mind. The guilt, the longing. And then, the incredibly engaging blue eyed, red headed firecracker that was waiting for him in California. No matter! He was not ejecting...

As he wandered away from the crash site, he was amazed at still being alive and congratulated himself for not bailing! A near miss. As was Jake's way, his brain switched from his near death memories to the problems at hand. Was he going to get court marshaled for crashing the million dollar U.S. Navy government issued Curtiss SB2C Helldiver? In the middle of nowhere, with severe shock setting in, he tried to concentrate on staying alive. One way was to get away from the Helldiver, after all, it was full of gas and could explode any second. But what was that rattling sound? Sounded like shooting and bullets hitting…..a couple days later 10,000 bullet cases were counted in the exact area of where Second Lieutenant Nelson E. Jacobs crashed his bomber.

Chapter 1 – September 1937

THE REJECTION

The Missouri Pacific Lines passenger car had a lulling affect; the gentle sway and the clickity-clack sound as it rolled along the tracks 254.5 miles from McGehee, Arkansas to Baton Rouge, Louisiana. The rhythm of the locomotive almost smoothed Jake's nerves, but not enough to alter his tension. Thoughts of this 19 year old graduate of McGehee Public High School were many and varied. He was on a course of life changing events but little did he know how enormous they were. His thoughts were on his future as a Louisiana State University football player as was nearly promised him by a scout that saw him play as the running back of his high school a year ago. He knew he had a natural talent for running and his agility was apparent on the field. As he leaned back for the last few miles before he stepped onto the Louisiana soil, he dreamt of making his football debut and he reminisced of the big moment when he, Duke the Devil Horse, made the play of the season running and dodging his way to a touchdown and into the conversations of every family dinner table in town. He was the hero, at least for a while! That was a big deal in a small town in America in the 1930's, a football hero that takes the local high school into the state championship. Yes sir, Duke the Devil Horse Jacobs was sure to be getting a scholarship to LSU. Or at least that is what he was made to believe. The train stopped, he got off. Doubt began to fill his brain. The football injury he sustained during his senior year seemed to be healed, but what if it wasn't healed enough? He had to get that out of his mind and think positive. He was a superb running back and he was made to believe he was one of the best in the country, the one for LSU. As he carried his possession packed battered suitcase across the train tracks to his destiny, he tried not to think about the people he left behind. Indeed, he will have time for that later. The mission at that moment was to make the LSU football team and to get an education while he was at it. But, some things were not to be! His football dream was turned down and without a scholarship to get an education, his 5'9" frame sat silently on the local bench next to the train tracks and the memories flooded him.

He wasn't sure which bothered him more, the abandonment of his mother or his girlfriend. Both were devastating. During World War I, a horrific flu was claiming millions of lives around the world. It was the Black Plague and most of its victims were child bearing aged women. His mother was one of them. After giving birth to Nelson Edward Jacobs on April 4, 1918 in Dumas, Arkansas his mother, Bessie, died from the plague leaving his father with a four month old infant. That should not have been news to him at the age of 19, but it was. He had just recently been told by his father that the woman who raised him, the person he called Mom, was not his birth mother but rather his mother's sister whom his father had married a couple years after his birth. The truth was out but the reality troubled him. He was shocked. He was angry. He felt betrayed and abandoned. Although given some time, he knew he would get over that feeling. He also knew he would never know his real mom and that would always haunt him. But, Jake being a quiet contemplator and driven to do what was necessary, decided not to dwell on it. What he needed to dwell on at this turning point in his life was the fact that he certainly could not go home so soon after being rejected by LSU. His emotions were almost out of control between the loss of his dream to play football and the other, more recent, abandonment.

There was his girlfriend, he called her Babe, only 17 years old, blue eyed, at 4'10" and she adored him. Jake's sister, Elizabeth, had introduced them the year before. As he sat on that lonely, cold bench at the train station with his hazel eyes staring at the tracks in front of him, his thoughts wondered back to Babe and the long walks around town with her; especially walking to the movies in the evenings, paying 30 cents to get in. He smiled to himself thinking of the atrocious price of 85 cents for the grand stand seats which he refused to pay. Then there was the expensive price he paid to take Babe to the performance at the 555 Ballroom to dance to the music of Tommy Dorsey. They had spent quite a lot of time together during the past year on her family's home front porch swing. That was the best time. Babe's father would come out now and then and ask for a cigarette. He knew Jake did not smoke. Even so, the black haired young gentleman would always shake his head and say, "No thank you, sir." There was a silent agreement between the men that ole' Dad was checking to make sure Jake didn't do any hanky-panky with his daughter. Of course, swinging on the porch swing did include cuddling and more. (So much more in fact, that he later admitted that leaving may have kept him from getting Babe "into trouble") They were young and in love as any young people of their ages could be. Jake thought their relationship was strong and exclusive but lately he had been wondering why the boy at the local market was delivering so many groceries to Babe's house and why he was hanging around her place so much? With a heavy heart about the affections of Babe waning, he packed his only possessions to set off to his football career at LSU, stopping briefly to say goodbye to Babe at her front porch.

Now, his LSU dream had vanished and going home to face his rejections was almost too much for him. The train should have been coming along anytime so he sat gathering his courage to board the train and sadly, with humiliating undertones, resolved to return to his home town and face his new found revelations. However, his life was just about to take a 180 degree turn, for better or worse!

Two military men approached him from the other side of the tracks. Heading directly toward him, he wondered who they were and what they wanted. He soon learned they were United States Marine Corps recruiters. He was the perfect profile of a young man that needed the Marines. He joined right there and then, not so much for the opportunity to serve the United States of America, but for a night in the local hotel and a hot home cooked meal at the nearby café. Whoever said the way to a man's heart is through his stomach? For Jake food was also a way to his commitments too. There were many things Jake could turn down, but food (and a controlling woman) was never one of them. On the fateful day of September 29, 1937 with a quiet comfortable room to sleep in and food in his stomach, he did not regret his decision to join the Marines, even when the two recruiters arrived the next morning to give him a train ticket to transport him directly to his boot camp of six weeks. America was not at war at this point, but things were heating up throughout the world. The Japanese had invaded China and were gaining territory and Germany was eyeing the small countries surrounding them, just waiting for the opportune time to invade. America needed not just a few good men, but thousands and Jake was one of them!

For a young man whose only previous responsibilities were to go to school, do well in football, and be kind to his 4 sisters and 2 brothers, the clickity-clack of the train to Beaufort, South Carolina was mostly relaxing. He quickly dismissed his thoughts of his siblings, for now he knew none of them were his full blood and he was not close to any of them anyway. His concerns were of his new life, whatever that meant! He felt he dodged a bullet by not having to go home and face the people he left earlier that week. He had a job. He wasn't quite sure what kind of a job, but once again Jake was not one to panic, so he just sat quietly thinking. He had made a commitment to the U.S. Marine Corp and he would honor that commitment.

Perris Island, the training center for the Marines, was to be his home for the next six weeks. He stood in line to claim ownership to his government issued metal bucket stuffed with toilet articles such as a straight edge razor, toothpaste, hand soap and other essentials. Then he started what would be his life for the next few weeks; following orders. He was rushed off to a long wooden two story barrack and was assigned a bunk on the first floor. As the day went on, all the bunks were filled and he was with the members of his training platoon. Marine Corporal Snuffy Smith set the tone by introducing himself and Sergeant Schmidt, "You belong to us until you are shipped out. Your training begins now so fallout and you will have supper. You will do nothing you are not told to do." Not friendly. Certainly not the kind of welcome Jake was use to in his small town in Arkansas. Ah well! At least he would get three square meals a day.

The training began at 5 am the next morning and consisted of close order drilling, use of rifles and pistols, first aid and lots of orders. It never ended. Right when the trainees thought there would be a break, there would be more orders. Non-relenting. Endless. Longest six weeks of his life. Perhaps, if he realized on that fateful night in Louisiana that Marines were trained for land, sea, and air, he would have reneged, but, something was coming alive in Jake. It certainly was not the jumping off the highest diving board the Marine Corps could find for their recruits. Jake did not like that, not at all. He seriously was contemplating not taking orders to jump. But, he was a Marine now. He jumped, survived and was thankful the Navy recruiters were not in Louisiana that fateful night guaranteeing Jake's "high dive" career to be repeated. Jake's feeling of "coming alive", perhaps, was the feeling of responsibility, doing the right thing, independence and certainly a sense of commitment and love for his country.

There was target practice with no ammunition. There would be no live ammunition until everyone was ready. Finally, the day came to go to the live fire range. No mistakes were permitted. In the pits "Maggie Draws" (misses) were more than frowned upon, they were forbidden. Finally, Jake's turn to shoot came. As he stood on the firing line, he felt himself internally shaking, but his quiet self determination scored him a 300; a sharp shooting qualification. "Not bad, but not too good either," he was thinking. He really wanted to be an expert. A man with great expectations for himself. However, his qualifications landed him a temporary assignment to Eighth and Eye Streets, Washington D.C. Another train ride! Now he had a job and no more Marine training camp. It could only get better. Once again, the clickity-clack and the swaying of the rail cars as he rolled along to his new destination, Jake continued to think. He thought about his destiny and he had accepted it.

More barracks, only the scenery was different. The hub of America and he could experience it. He experienced it as a telephone operator which had direct lines to the White House. What a great way to know what was happening. Between listening to the current affairs of the world, Jake filled his spare time reading the Arkansas Gazette at the Library of Congress, visiting famous monuments, discovering the downtown business district and soaking up as much information and history as he could absorb. He experienced the excitement of learning and wanted to experience as much as possible during his military career. He received that chance on one warm morning in 1938 when the barracks First Sergeant came in and said, "Marine, I have your orders, pack up all your gear, clear the post." He headed to the Navy Yard main gate with his sea bag packed. As he looked out over the water of the Potomac River passing George Washington's home of Mount Vernon, the overnight ferry carried him to Norfolk, Virginia to await the arrival of the USS Chaumont, the ship that would take him to China.

Chapter 2 – Slow Boat to China

A few years after the Great War, the United States Navy sent Marines to China on two transports, the USS Henderson and the USS Chaumont. The USS Henderson was nicknamed "Hendy Maru" and was the most popular of the two ships. Hampton Roads, Virginia, an ice free body of water, was the port of departure for these two military ships. They would run along the East coast, pass through the Panama Canal and veer up the western coast of the United States and then cross over to Hawaii, Guam and Manila. Then the route would change direction heading northwest along the Chinese coast of Shanghai, Peking and Chinwangtao. Both transports made stops along the way to pick up and drop off troops or supplies. These two US Naval vessels would take about one month to make the trip each way and each would make two complete trips each year.

Jake boarded the nineteen year old USS Chaumont for an incredibly slow ride to his destination, Peking. He should have been nervous about the long trip over the ocean for he had never been one to be on the water. Living in McGhee, he relished his days of playing on the banks of the Mississippi River, but never did he get his feet wet with any kind of boating. This was a new adventure. He would have worried about getting seasick or the tensions between the Japanese and the Chinese, but his mind was on an important personal matter, his letter from Babe. He had received it two days before he and his regiment were to board the ship and his heart soared! Babe loved him and would wait for him promising him her heart always. Who cared what happened to him now? His only goal was to survive so he could return to Arkansas and put a ring on Babe's finger. And so, when it was time to board the USS Chaumont, he gleefully stepped into the motorized whale boat to be taken out to the ship. From the deck of the ship, cargo nets were dropped down so the enlisted passengers could climb aboard. With no training on climbing cargo nets, Jake clumsily struggled with his footing but with determination and athleticism on his side, finally made it on deck with a lot of jeering from his peers. No matter! He was in love and he was going off to see the world. What could possibly go wrong?

Hunkering down in his third lower deck bunk, he was ready for the duties that were expected from him for the next 90 days, a much longer trip than usual for the Chaumont. There were stops to be made along the way; a lot of stops. Realizing this, Jake took the initiative to go directly to the ship's First Sergeant and asked to be assigned the duty of messenger since there was no automated method of locating individuals. His request was accepted and he was ordered to the bridge immediately where upon the Chief Quartermaster ordered him to take the mid watch. It was the perfect job for the man with a continuous empty, iron clad stomach because for the next 90 days, he was to make certain the crew on the bridge never lacked for coffee or food, especially the freshly baked bread from the ship's galley. His life was good. He had clinched a position of being in charge of food and his Arkansas love was home waiting for him. He made sure that he would keep his assignment on this transport until they reached their Far Eastern destination remembering to implement hard work, be on time and a lot of "Yes sirs". He was getting the knack of the military. Very easy, direct, precise! Just like Jake liked it. As the pilot guided the Chaumont out of Hampton Roads, the Captain took command. Jake grinned as the vessel began to pick up its flank speed of 10 knots. How good it felt to have fresh homemade bread from the ship's galley and letters from his girl!

First stop, Gitmo, Cuba. The lease of 1903 gave the United States of America Guantanamo Bay Naval Base, GTMO, "complete jurisdiction and control" while giving the Republic of Cuba "the ultimate sovereignty". Luckily, in 1938, no one on board of the Chaumont could have imagined the challenges that specific lease would cause in the future. As Jake was given liberty and left the ship to check out his land legs, he and his fellow Marines excitedly went to explore the sandy beaches, the few existing buildings, and a Chinese restaurant. With disappointment, they reported back to the bridge of the ship 12 hours early with Jake exclaiming, "We fought the Spanish American War for this?" They spent their off time duty playing cards. At this point none of them could fully understand the strategic placement of GTMO for the future of America, and why would they? It was only 1938.

Panama City, Panama was more disappointing than Cuba only because this was one of America's territories. The

Panama Canal connected the Eastern Hemisphere with the West. It allowed transit of boats to make a huge short cut, a 2000 mile plus short cut. How awesome was that? If only Columbus and a few others had that advantage. As Jake eagerly left on liberty, he once again expected great things. Again, disappointment ensued. The city was filthy, beggars filled the streets and the feelings of desperation were evident as each Marine was interrogated, "You want whiskey or girl?" Enough was enough. Jake headed back to the ship ahead of schedule and awaited the passage through the canal the following morning. A young Marine with small town Arkansas values realized world cultures were not easily related to. He would not forget his last two stops. Never.

With Balboa, Panama ahead, he had seriously considered not taking liberty. He had written a letter to his beloved that day describing the poverty and hopelessness of Panama City. In their lifetime the Panama Canal was an accomplishment for trade throughout the world and it was an American success story of political diplomacy as well as proof of American ingenuity. After all, we did help to win World War I! As Jake read Babe's reply to his heartfelt letter about the new cultures and worlds he had been exposed to, he was disgruntled. Her tone about what he saw was not disbelief, but the feeling of her not caring about his observations of other people in foreign places. Oh well, women! She didn't need to understand the turmoil of lands she had not been to, she still loved him and that was the important thing to him.

Jake decided to take a look around Balboa since they

were docked for a day. It was such a relief to see a city so opposite of the past two he had seen. Balboa, Panama was so clean, so American. He began to realize at the ripe young age of 19 years old the true values of America. Where America had influence, it showed. As Jake wondered about Balboa, he noticed the cleanliness and the definite presence of the American culture. He felt comfortable. But, his tour to China had just begun and so did his cultural awareness.

As the ship docked at each port and Naval Base along its way to Peking, supplies or enlisted men were dropped off or brought on. Each place was so different. Jake was in a world of his own. Being a thinker, he pondered everyone's actions and began to imagine their lives. He became intuitive and that gift would stay with him until the end of his life. He was never judgmental and he was a man of few words. He began to realize he had a purpose, but he really did not know what that purpose was.

Whew! American soil. San Diego! Jake was feeling like he made a great decision to join the Marines. Now, it was true that boats on the open waters of the Pacific Ocean were worse to get use to than the clickity-clack of a train, but the ports were beautiful with lots of time off and since Jake had not yet experienced any hostile countries, he valued his time on the streets. He was also experiencing people on American soil catering to his needs as a Marine which included respect. That felt good! He told himself to not get used to this supreme treatment because things would probably change. He was right.

As the Chaumont glided from San Diego to a fumigation of the ship at San Francisco, Jake was becoming more and more comfortable with his sea legs as the military vessel veered its way to Hawaii. He was tickled that he was seeing the America he had read about back in his little hometown of 2,500 people. What a great country. However, a very large, cold, hostile Pacific Ocean still laid ahead and so did the American territories, the Pacific Islands, and a foreign land that was experiencing unrest due to Japan's needs for its resources.

President Franklin D Roosevelt's Executive order in 1934 placed Wake Island and Midway under the Department of the Navy. They were isolated unincorporated territories of the United States strategically located as mid-Pacific refueling and emergency landing stops. The Chaumont made such a stop obtaining supplies and refueled. Then off to two more strategically located islands, Guam and the Philippines. They had become US territories after the Spanish American War. Stopping at the Guam Naval Station for a pickup of a few more Marines, Jake noticed an impressive Marine Captain that had come aboard. He later learned it was Chesty Puller, a famous fighter from the U.S. Central American Wars. He was on his way to join the 4th Marine Division in Shanghai. One day Jake was tired of staying in his hot, dimly lit, overcrowded quarters on the third deck below the main deck. Not on duty for the time being, he went onto the bridge to breathe some fresh air, drink a cup of coffee from the plentiful supply always available and listen to the information from the adjacent radio shack. He found he could learn a lot of what was happening on board as well as military information airing from ship to base to ship. Listening had become an important skill for him. Listen, learn, obey orders. Very important; especially for a young Marine.

Manila proved to be a brief stop with Hong Kong also quick. Nothing seemed very interesting to Jake, probably because he knew the next stop was Shanghai. He had heard rumors and some chattering from the ship's radio about Japanese military in those areas. Things were heating up, but he had no idea how much. He steadied his nerves by observing and listening and becoming prepared mentally. Those were his tools. He could not react in a negative, erratic way. That would be stupid. And besides, he was a Marine and the motto was "Semper Fidelis", always faithful. And he was.

After passing by Taiwan, the Captain headed up the mouth of the muddy Wampoo River. Heading for the predestinated location across from the "Bund", Shanghai's business area, the Marines who were scheduled to debark did so quickly into waiting trucks for transport to the 4th Marine Division Headquarters. Jake was not one of them. He did notice a familiar face leaving the ship, Chesty Puller. Since the Lieutenant had boarded ship, Jake kept his eyes and ears open so he could satisfy his curiosity of who this man was. A Virginian by birth, this thick-chested, tough, boisterous man enlisted into the Corps on August 1, 1918. He rose to the rank of captain as a jungle fighter in the Haitian outfit. Having earned two Navy Crosses in 1924 he had a reputation of having an intimidating appearance with a strong stance and a belligerent personality. He expected from himself the same as he expected from his men. Chesty loved a fight. Jake was in awe over this giant of a personality and when he heard Captain Puller's motto, "Be a model of valor by example and precept" Jake decided that was a good way to live life. Of course, he first contemplated this motto and used ole' Webster to find the meaning of "precept", (behavior). At the time, Jake had no idea that he and Chesty would meet again and continue the lesson.

As the harbor pilot guided the Chaumont out into the open ocean from the Wampoo River, the vessel headed towards the North China Sea. All crew members were at their stations and ready to begin the last leg of their lengthy journey. When the transport arrived at the ice free port of Chinwantao that was built by the British Mining Interest, it was steered to the easiest entry and up to a long pier. This was the end of the voyage for Marines remaining on board, including Jake. This was his stop, but not his destination. He didn't know that until the gangplank was lowered, everyone swarmed to the pier, and Corporal Henry took command. The Corporal's duty was to safely escort the Marines as well as embassy and civilian passengers to Peking. The key words to Jake were "safely" and "escort". Was there danger lurking? As the old coal burning engine pulled the train into the station with fading letters painted on its side "British Mining Company", Jake noticed the four old style passenger cars with five freight cars attached. The Corporal corralled the embassy and civilian passengers aboard the first cars while the Marines were ordered to board the remainder. As soon as the cars were loaded, the trip to Peking would begin. Rations would be provided onboard after the train began to move. Jake was so hungry by then, he was ecstatic to hear the word "rations". It wasn't fresh bread, but as he would learn during his time in China, rations would sometimes taste just as good. There were 40 Marines all told and they were assigned to duties. Some were posted guards on the cargo rail cars which contained six months of needed supplies for the Marine garrison and to last until the next supply ship arrived. Jake, not assigned to the first guard duty, settled into the uncomfortable old style European seat and watched as the countryside went past. Not much to see yet. The most interesting items were the armed Japanese guards at every stream and road crossing. Since the Japanese had invaded China by this time, they were in clear presence. Each Japanese guard was armed with a rifle with a bayonet making him look larger than he was. All were at attention as the train went by, not moving at all like the guards protecting Buckingham Palace in London. How strange that seemed. They looked more like statues rather than like humans. Jake was just beginning to sense the danger of being a Marine in a foreign country, especially in 1938.

The train moved over the rugged terrain and through small villages for a full day until dusk. Jake whispered to himself, "This place don't show me much," a phrase he would continue to use throughout his life. With the sound of the train whistle, the screeching of the brakes and the slowing of the clickity-clack, the train stopped at the dimly lit Peking station. Two Marine corporals came aboard and ushered the incoming replacements into columns of four and marched them out into the streets and through Peking's inner walls to what would become Jake's next new home, the Marine Barracks in Peking. Smelling food signaled his long journey to China had come to an end. Chow time! After bunk assignments were made, the forty marines had a good night's sleep without the rock of the ocean, the crashing of the waves, or the dimly lit, unventilated decks of the ship suffocating them. Orders were to be given at 6:00 am the following morning.

Chapter 3 -- Peking, China

The United States Marine Corps in China had a very unique set of challenges as compared to other parts of the world in the 1930's. Relations between Japan and the United States were deteriorating and the Marines were stuck in the middle. The mission for these China Marines was to protect U.S. interests. The most famous isolated detachments of leathernecks in Marine history were those posted as Guards at the Embassy at Peking. Of course, the newly recruited Marines that landed in Peking on that day in late 1938, had no real perception of the politics of the region at that time, including Jake. What he did realize was reveille began at 0630 hours by a college educated field musician that sounded his well practiced bugle in the stairwell of the second floor of the barracks. With 15 minutes to wash, dress, grab his weapon and fall in for breakfast at 0700 and just to make sure all the Marines made it in time, roll call. The first day was filled with weapon drills, physical examinations, and orders to check the company bulletin board each day for the list of daily activities. It sounded to Jake like a summer camp protocol, but he, of course, knew it would be much different; especially the orders and the stern, serious bellows of the officers. Also, the equipment was certainly much more heavy duty. Each man received a 1903 caliber 30-rifle with a strict warning to not lose it or misplace it. It was even considered a Marine's best friend. Instructions were to not let your personal houseboy touch it. "What? Repeat that?"

thought Jake! (He never would have asked the question, but what houseboy?) As his thoughts refocused on the matter at hand, the rifle, he caught the words "Always have it in formation and never forget the number of your rifle." He was glad he heard that, it seemed like a very serious order. Then, since the issuance of weapons was over, it was time to acquire a winter fur cap that also must be on you during each formation. A gun and a hat! Mmmm. Interesting equipment but probably necessary! But, there was more to come, the necessary acquaintance with the company weapons – 30-caliber machine gun, Browning Automatic Rifle (BAR) and a Thomason 45 caliber sub-machine gun. The next order from the senior officer, "You will qualify on all weapons", caught Jake by surprise as he began to realize the fact that those Japanese in China just might be more of a challenge and threat than he or his fellow Marines first thought. With the last order of the day, "Do not let your native house boy clean your weapon!" they were dismissed. Once again, what house boy? He was filled in by other Marines that had been in Peking for a while that there were house boys to clean your bunk area, your clothing, and anything else you wanted them to do. Basically, a butler kind of a guy. Sounded good to Jake! Just don't let them touch your weapon. Why would he?

The next day brought him guard duty, then came Guard Mount. Remembering his uniform, weapon and the knowledge of the orders that had to be carried out to perfection, Jake began his scheduled duty. The tours of guard duty were four hours, however, ones not on duty had to remain in the guard house until his relief reported and began his duty. Jake's first post was on top of the inner wall of the city beginning at 2400 hours (midnight) and 0600 (6am). Post Number 3, atop the wall extending from the guardhouse atop the wall for about 400 yards and return. To contact the sergeant of the guard one had to crank a two handed cranked field telephone which was located at each end of the guard post. On the wall, a good portion of the city had visibility at night, but it gave off an eerie feeling.

Within a couple weeks on night guard duty on the wall, Jake heard rapid gun fire. Rushing to the nearest field telephone, he frantically rang up the sergeant on duty to report the shots. With the assurance from the sergeant to, "Take it easy. It happens all the time; just another fight between the "Japs" and Chinese. Just keep your eyes open." Jake, rattled and shaken by the gunshots so close, began to get the picture how his life was taking a turn and it was more important than ever to be diligent, attentive, and to stay qualified on all weapons. His fur hat came in handy too. It kept him warm as he guarded the wall and pondered about everything in his life. Just another part of his personal training to become intuitive.

Guard duty was not always on the wall, sometimes, it was to guard a prisoner in the stockade. The prisoner was confined with only bread and water for misconduct. Actually, Jake thought this was a better duty than the dark wall with guns shooting at who knows what. Always knowing that taking orders was not an option, he personally had a chance to see the misery of the misconduct charge of not doing what you were told as a Marine. Stockade? No thanks!

Post #1 was the main gate to the Embassy. Being a sentry on duty was tiresome. He soon learned he was synonymous to the British Tommy's and the Japanese he observed from the train; one had to maintain at an attention position for the duration of the 4-hour guard duty. Being selected because of his ability to maintain a positive attitude and to portray a demeanor of a professional serious soldier, Jake stood at attention as the Embassy guard being relieved by another carefully selected Marine who marched at attention to the post to relieve him. Jake figured it was better than wall duty or stockade duty. Embassy Guard duty suited him fine. It gave him time to think without gunshots or idle talking by prisoners to distract him. And besides, Embassy guards when off duty, were granted liberty and excused from routine duties except for field exercises and range firing and those, as any Marine would admit, could keep you alive. Jake's personality and natural abilities were beginning to pay off: stone face, few words, loyal, smart.

Liberty meant Jake could go on sight-seeing excursions on bicycles and sometimes rickshaws. Always these trips were of short duration but long enough to go into the shopping areas. As he wondered about, the Japanese soldiers were searching Chinese buildings. Camel trains would enter the city through the Hatamin Street Gate. He often wandered what the contents were that they were bringing in from out of nowhere. Even the Japanese soldiers on duty at the gate seemed to wonder about their loads but they never interfered with their progress. The gate was near the Fox Tower where major fighting occurred. During the Boxer Rebellion, this was the scene where American soldiers fought the Boxers. The result of that rebellion was the Quing Dynasty ended and China became a Republic. The Americans were rewarded for their valor during that scrimmage which is the main reason why China allowed American presence in their country.

Street vendors were selling their hot food from their hand drawn carts. The divine smells would draw Jake to the carts and although Jake was tempted, he decided not to indulge. That was the reason his excursions were short, he had to get some food that would be safe to eat back at the barracks. He couldn't risk getting some kind of dysentery and lose his guard post! Also, in the vicinity of the Fox Tower, were small hand cultivated farms using human waste for fertilizers carried in from the city in "Honey Buckets" carried across their shoulders on "Yo Ho" poles It was always best to detour around those areas and just another reason not to eat locally grown food. Sometimes during field exercises, the Marines would pass near a cluster of local farms. Needless to say, they wasted no time to pass through those smelly, unsanitary areas.

Liberty would also take the China Marines past and sometimes into an establishment which was a gentleman's club controlled by a burly white Russian male watching every move every American male made. This was a place the Marines would go to relax with a drink, chat with friends and sometimes relax with one of the Russian Princesses. Going to the cabaret was not a habit of Jakes, although a friend of his, Dave, would stop by often just to hear the local gossip. Jake thought the cabarets were trouble. His opinion stemmed from his experience of bike rides around the city from the Point of Invasion of 400,000 Japanese soldiers to the Summer Places. On one specific bike trip, he decided to stop and eat lunch at a well known local Russian eating place. As he ordered his lunch, he looked up to see two huge Russians approaching him. They were from the Alkzar body guards for the white Russian Princesses. Time to leave! Interestingly enough, although Jake did not realize it at that moment, one of his most intriguing and fun memories would take place in a China cabaret.

The US Marines assignment in Peking continued to be to safeguard American lives, property and commerce in the great city itself and, also in the Yangtze River valley as well. As The Chinese government obsessed over anti-communist threats, it ignored a bigger threat at the time, the Japanese. Peking and the surrounding areas were becoming more vulnerable by the day, and the Marines were beginning to sense it. Company B, Jake's outfit, was ordered to spend two weeks on the live firing range. Each Marine must qualify on each weapon. When not firing, they were assisting. Jake fired his 06 rife, the BAR caliber 45 automatic pistol and the 30-caliber machine gun and demonstrated use of the bayonet. He qualified on all weapons including sharpshooter with his rifle. Yippee! An extra dollar pay increase just for being a sharpshooter. More money and a better chance of staying alive if he ever had to use it in combat! So much for the training and extra pay! Back to Embassy Guard duty! 4 hours on, 8 hours off! Jake went back to his usual get it done, don't complain, professional attitude. He guarded, contemplated and composed his next letter to Babe who consistently sent him letters of love and loyalty!

Tests were coming up for promotions and Jake was on the list. He was relieved of his guard duty to study until tests were completed. Jake didn't like tests, but it was a break from the boredom of guard duty. And a possible promotion couldn't hurt his pay or his ego! More money to save for the wedding ring. So study he did and at promptly 0800 the following Monday he took the test. He returned to his Post #1, Main gate to the Embassy. On November 28, 1939 he unexpectedly was relieved by another sentry so he could report to Col. A.H. Turndee's office. There he was officially promoted to Private First Class. Jake, stone faced, respectfully exited the office feeling great! Promotion number one challenge had been met.

The knowledge of Hitler's invasion of Poland three months prior and, the growing Japanese presence in China was on everyone's mind. What will happen next? Jake felt he needed to make a transfer to the Fourth Marines in Shanghai so he could make a bigger difference for America. Requests could be made after 15 months at one duty station in China. He qualified. He put in the request for transfer and waited.

Two weeks later on a warm afternoon while playing

a pick-up baseball game on the barracks field, Jake was summoned to the first sergeant's office. Orders were given to pack his gear, clear his post and with a "good luck Marine" was transferred to the Fourth Marines in Shanghai. With his sea bag packed, he cleared the post and secured his weapon. Then, with a few other Marines he boarded the clickity-clack train, passed all the Japanese guards at attention and boarded the USS Henderson for the short three day journey to Shanghai. Time for Jake to write a pride filled, thoughtful letter to his girl in Arkansas.

Chapter 4 ---- December 1939 – Transfer to Fourth Headquarter, Shanghai

The Fourth Headquarter in Shanghai, China was a highly respected Marine combat unit and Jake was part of it. Across from the primary business district of China and the largest docks, the USS Henderson anchored in the Whangpu River. As the U.S. military transport ship was securing its position in the harbor, Jake felt a pang of hesitation. However, he quickly discarded it and debarked with the other Marines that had been transferred. He was assigned to the Fourth 2nd Battalion. Clutching his sea bag and his weapon, Jake climbed aboard a USML truck along with a dozen of his peers that had also transferred down from North China and was driven down the Bubbling Well Road past the newly completed Marine Club and onto the 2nd battalion compound. First sergeants gathered together their newly assigned replacements. Duke was the only transferred Marine in the group to be assigned to "H" company which was the machine gun company for the Battalion.

The friendly greeting from First Sergeant Morse was sincere but full of vital information. Explaining the difference in the equipment of the North China water cooled 50 caliber guns versus the air cooled ones used in Shanghai, Jake listened intently. Since the assignment of the 4th Marines in Shanghai were to patrol the international settlement protecting American lives, property and commerce, all of the

Corps must always be alert to danger. Interestingly, the firing range was a place for competition with fellow marines in the regiment and held in high esteem. The competition did not just include weaponry but track. To outdo other regimental units was the key to being a Fourth Headquarter Marine in China. "Pride and success means a lot here and with people like "Chesty Puller" you better give it your best. In fact, you had better remember we expect 110% effort at all times." And with that comment, the Sergeant ordered Jake to be taken to his quarters. What kind of a combat unit had he gotten himself into? The Marines are known for their expertise in combat, but competing amongst themselves gave the men a certain feeling of belonging and kept them alert. Jake decided he liked that. He was after all, an athlete. He liked to win.

Live fire exercises on the range pursued for ole' Jake until the company clerk informed him of the fact that the company needed good runners. Obviously, records were reviewed because he never talked about his high school career as a running back in football or his track records. He was fast. It seemed natural for him. Being a mere 5'9", his legs weren't that long, but his athleticism and his determination made up for that. His legs were meant to move and to move fast. Somehow, this regiment of competitive officers knew that. He was to report at the American School to work out on their track the next day at 1400 hours. No longer was Jake training in live fire weaponry, he was training in running. Somehow, the First Sergeant needing his quick feet had convinced the battalion Sergeant Major that PFC Jacobs could fill in as is needed for a squadron leader more than company "H" needed him. So, PFC Jacobs had become a member of "E" Company with a potential promotion to squadron leader before he returned from his first day of track training. Not only was he reassigned to new quarters and a new squadron, he had in fact become the acting Squadron leader of the platoon of "E" company. Better than that was all his equipment had been moved for him, and moved into a single room. No more loud snores, smelling companions talking in their sleep. Just him! Alone! And a list of his newly assigned squadron. Too good to be true. Got to write Babe about this! Looks like running track was going to replace shooting at the Japs. He was feeling good about getting home in one piece!

Regiment titles were not to be dismissed lightly! Jake immediately went to his quarters and addressed his newly assigned squadron . Being the youngest Marine present, it seemed to be a set up for a joke, but it wasn't. He took charge, gave a very short speech including the words, "I need you but you need me more, so let us make a go of it." Being a well bred Southern boy, he thanked all the guys. Soft spoken, to the point, controlled! Yes, Jake was coming into his own as a young gentleman and a true Marine. And all he had to do at that point was help the 2nd Battalion win the Regimental title. They did. Jake went on to win the 440 m. at the annual police meet at the local racetrack sponsored by the local police. The 4th Precinct won four first places and became a force in local track Shanghai events. Since there were no Olympics that year, the International community made their own. It was the China National Games. Jake won the Gold Medal in the 440! Jake was truly feeling his oats, but was not a bragger by any stretch of the imagination. He was humble, strong, pleased! Shortly after the National Olympics of 1940, Jake took the promotion test for Corporal. He placed 8th out of 40 and was promoted on November 6, 1940 on his first enlistment. No more standing in lines; he could go directly to the NCO mess hall! Ahhhh. Life was good for Jake until he got a letter in the mail.

It was after a satisfying Marine breakfast and he was thinking how nice it was to be in Shanghai away from the Northern part of China. He no longer needed to dress with his fur hat, just his weapon! Yes, life was good. He was excitedly waiting to hear from Babe and was ecstatic when a letter had arrived for him. It was from Arkansas but the handwriting and return address was different. On edge, he ripped the letter open in fear something was wrong. He was right. Something was wrong; very wrong. The letter was from Babe's mother informing him of events in Babe's life that meant he could no longer write her. As he read the letter his hands began to shake, his eyes blurred. He was a Marine damn it, he had to be strong, courageous, endure, survive even if he didn't want to at the time. He quietly got out a match, struck it, and applied the flame to that fatal letter…. he watched it burn in the dirt beneath him until it was ashes. Then he rubbed his foot into it making sure not an ember was left. Not even a little tiny spark…because the spark was gone. Babe was gone. He could not write to her because she was married and had a baby! Her mother stopped the communication, not Babe. Deceit! He was right! His intuition had told him when he last saw her that she had someone else. That was one reason why he could not go back to McGehee. But she wrote to him, deceived him... Put it out of your mind, Jake. Move on. Forget. A near miss to marry someone like that! With no words to anyone, he repressed his feelings, his memories. With great effort and loyalty to the US Marine Corps and to his country he began to make new plans for himself. The few. The Proud. The Marines. Always Faithful.

Jake was transferred for the third time within the 2nd Battalion soon after his devastating letter. He was to assist the Company Platoon leader. He moved into the apartment located over the main entrance to the compound. He could not believe his luck or his eyes. The company was billeted there. Wow. A fireplace and a direct telephone. Jake soon learned that this was a favorite hideout for Major Chesty Puller, now Chief Executive Officer and Commanding Officer of the battalion. What a man to learn from. Jake could not see in the future, so he had no idea he was under the leadership of one of the most decorated members of the military in history. Puller retired in 1955 as a lieutenant general with 5 Navy Crosses and one Army Distinguished Service cross. All for valor. Jake learned a great deal about the Corps lore and about Chesty himself. He also was reinforced by Chesty's motto, "Be a model of valor by example and precept" and vowed to have the same motto to guide him throughout his life in whatever endeavor he decided to encounter. Jake was the corporal under Chesty Puller's command. Expectations were high. Equipment consisted of field telephone wire carts, and signal flares. There were no radios then. On field exercises wire had to be laid between field locations and retrieved upon conclusion of exercises; not always an easy task, but what are corporals made for? This job kept his mind off his personal woes and allowed enough time to satisfy some of his needs at a local cabaret located in the International Community. Along with his promotions came more pay and since he didn't need a ring anymore, why not spend it on some down time within the White Russian cabaret that was so popular with the U.S. Marine? A cabaret was a good spot to listen to local political talk, get a drink, and relax with a beautiful white Russian princess. Why not? He was single and needy! A memory he decided not to repress. Life was getting better for Jake.

It was November of 1940 and Jake had been stationed in China for three years. It was time to return to the states. His time in Shanghai was of mixed emotions but with more and more Japanese tensions and border invasions, he began to feel the eyes on him. It was a strange and uneasy feeling; people watching his every move as he patrolled in huge, dark, silent buildings every night. Fortunately, orders to depart to the east coast of the United States on the USS Chaumont came in. He had only two weeks left in China. Several of his Marine buddies stood on the deck wishing him luck on his next assignment. His time in Asia was quickly coming to a final close. Or was it? Something kept nagging at Jake. Was he being intuitive again? He boarded the USS Chaumont on February 18, 1941 just months before all Marines in China were withdrawn by orders of the President of the United States due to Japanese alliance with the Axis Powers. Great Britain had withdrawn all her troops and interest in China months before due to the invasion by Hitler in Europe. She needed the resources in Great Britain to protect the homeland. Japan would have total control in China and the International Community by the end of 1941. A near miss for Jake!

Chapter 5 – Stateside

On board the transport vessel once again, Jake bid farewell to half a dozen of marines that gathered to wish him goodbye from the 4th Marines, 2nd Battalion. They wished Corporal Jacobs the best of luck at his new assignment, whatever it was. This time he did not have to climb the cargo net which he was very thankful for since his fellow marines once again would have jeered at him. That would have been more humiliating than the first time when he was a mere private. For all the new skills Jake had learned during his time as a China Marine, climbing cargo nets was not one of them. Once on board he spotted Corporal Burns who had worked in the company office of the Peking Detachment. Corporal Burns was from Tennessee and across the Mississippi River from Jake's Arkansas. They were both headed to Norfolk Navy Yard for further assignment. With travel orders in hand, Jake went topside prior to the ship's departure from Shanghai's Bund into the Whangpu River channel with the course set to Manila in the Philippines; arrival to be three days later. Little did he know that once they arrived in Manila, not in three but in five days, the return voyage to the United States had been delayed 10 days due to the USS Chaumont's change in orders. Rumors were rampant. Jake and Burns brainstormed what could have happened in the world, after all, Japan was taking over territory quickly in the Pacific Theater and Hitler was a madman taking over Europe. As the China 4th Marines disembarked, Jake did not.

He was destined to be elsewhere. But where? The Baatan Death March April 10, 1942, occurred less than a year later. 650 American Prisoners of War died in the hands of the cruel Japanese. He was not one of them... a near miss, again!

Eventually, the ship sailed up the Olongapo to the North, taking several days to pick up cargo and one sailor scheduled to be transported to the naval prison state-side. It then began its return to the states. Jake, hoping for his bridge side assignment of messenger, was not so lucky. No longer could he control the flow of fresh baked bread and coffee to the bridge and himself. He was assigned guard duty of the prisoner. He and one of the USS Chaumont's sailors would rotate guarding the prisoner and since there was no brig, the prisoner would be locked in a paint locker for the entire return ship. Oh dread! The duty began as soon as the prisoner was on ship and the two guards relieved each other in eight hour shifts. So, the return voyage back to the U.S. was not a pleasant one for Jake who was not a seaman or a prison guard at heart to begin with, but with 8 hours between any kind of duty, Jake found coffee, fresh bread, fresh sea air and he even found a place to relax so that he could do what he did best; listen, observe, contemplate, in other words, eavesdrop on the radio room.

The route back to the states was the same route as outbound. The best stop was Hawaii when Jake finally was relieved of his prison duty. The imprisoned sailor was loaded off and turned over to the Fleet Command. Since the last leg of the journey was to Vallejo, California, Duke and Burns made plans to meet in Memphis, Tennessee after their 30 day leave and proceed to Norfolk together. Jake, with nothing much to do with his 30 day leave, decided to enjoy the sea air, the beautiful coast line of the Pacific Ocean as viewed from California, and he realized what a relaxing, open environment the western United States offered. In hopes that someday he would be assigned to the West Coast of America he clickity-clacked his way by train to Memphis to meet up with his friend and then to Norfolk to receive his orders. He did not stop in Arkansas, in fact, he bypassed it completely. No reason to stop there and muster up those feelings. He had no desire to touch base with family or with the person who dumped him. Jake was fine tuning his ability to put negative past experiences out of his mind. Some would call that repressing, Jake called it surviving. One thing Jake knew; he wanted to stay a Marine and as soon as September 18, 1941 came around he would let the Corps know his intentions. Once in Norfolk, Burns' orders were to join the Fleet Marine Forces and he was to report to Quantico while Jake was ordered to the Washington Navy Yard. The Navy Yard was familiar as was the Marine barracks at Eighth and I Street in Southeast Washington D.C. Upon signing in, Jake was advised that he would be in charge of all permanent gates and would have about 60 Marines under his command. The permanent gates not only included every gate in and out of the Navy Yard but also, in and out of the White House. Of course, this caused some dissension due to his rank, but being a China Marine it seemed to elevate one's ability. Go figure! Worked for Jake!

Jake put his usual effort into his assignment; diligence, professionalism, hard work. Maybe the new China-made uniform had something to do with the assignment! When not on guard duty, he had to establish a schedule for the time the guards time off from gate duty. The job was in and out processing daily of thousands of civilian employees. One of his friends, a retired Navy Chief that was stationed in the civilian workforce, offered his knowledge and help such as if President Roosevelt was coming down to spend the weekend. He would call so that he could have his Marines in dress uniforms and positioned to salute the President. Another time, he asked if Jake would train a civilian security force for the New Naval Hospital located in Bethesda, Maryland. This he did and as a result the bond between the chief and him grew tighter. His work partnership was so tight with the chief it did in fact help to get immediate assistance when needed and it helped to provide a more secure defense plant for the forthcoming armed conflict.

Not only did Jake do an enthusiastic and diligent job, he also was an excellent observer and knew when to talk and when not to. These were exemplary traits for a Marine guard at the White House. The things he saw made him ponder for many years. For example, Roosevelt would go to the boat docks quite regularly and was met by a young woman (not his wife). What was going on? (History would prove that a lot was going on.)Unfortunately, not all of his duties were intriguing. One evening as he was just finishing a cup of coffee and settling in to listen to some relaxing modern 40's music on the radio, a call came to him to report back to his position immediately. Quickly he dressed into his uniform and rushed to find White House security telling him the situation. What he was ordered to do was to pick up a body of a man that had jumped from a tall, elite hotel building of Washington, D.C. He shuddered when he heard the man's name but he did not show his concern. He knew this was a "secret" job, never to be told to anyone. He went to the lifeless body, picked it up, delivered it to the authorities that were specified, went back home, had a quick beer (who wouldn't?) and went to bed, never to speak of it. Yes, Jake was the trusted one. A China Marine with a closed mouth.

September 19, 1941 arrived with his Honorable Discharge. On it was, "Character: excellent. Service: Honest and Faithful. Recommended for reappointment." With a sigh of relief, Jake knew he was accepted to "re up" in the Marines. He continued with his job protecting the White House and the Naval Base by monitoring the comings and goings of every single person. Then the unbelievable happened, the "day in infamy" (President Roosevelt) came, December 7, 1941 the day Pearl Harbor was struck by Japan. As every American tuned in their radios to hear of this horrific event, the military tightened their security. Not only was Pearl Harbor hit, the Japanese forcibly took control of the Philippines, Guam, the Marshall Islands and China. For every bad thing in Jake's life prior to the moment he heard of the attack, none was as deblorable and frightening than December 7, 1941. He was officially enlisted in the U.S. Marines for his second stint on December 9, 1941. He would help America. He would die if he had to for everything that America stood for! After two more promotions, one on January 8, 1942 to Sergeant and the other on July, 1, 1942 to Platoon Sergeant which gave him more pay and more responsibility, Jake was feeling that guarding Washington D.C. was not enough. He could do more, but what? The answer came on the day a hundred or so Naval Air Cadets reported to the Marine barracks for primary training at the local Naval air station. It was his first contact with Naval Air. As Jake watched these young enthusiastic cadets, his thoughts took him back in time to Arkansas when he was a teenager when boys were allowed to wonder the wildernesses and country sides of their homes with no worries from their parents. The 30's were hard times for most people in the United States due to the Great Depression and the Dust Bowl, but Jake never felt it, nor did he remember "hard" times. His father was a lawyer, one time Mayor of his birth city, Dumas, Arkansas, and owned a saw mill. Although Jake later recalled the saw mill slowed down and lost some business during the Great Depression, it never affected the financial situation of the family. It didn't affect Jake. He never had to work during his years at home except chores now and then and to be respectful to people of authority such as his father and mother and to be kind to his four sisters and two brothers. As he thought about his siblings, he got a feeling of sadness; he now knew none of them were his full blood. He immediately dismissed this part of his past and put his mind back on the good times;

school, football, running track and barnstorming. As Jake reminisced, he embraced the fondest memory of his boy hood as a barnstormer with his cousin, Willy Meeks. Willy owned a one engine Ryan airplane, the same kind Lindberg flew across the Atlantic in 1927 although Willy's was not modified like The Spirit of St. Louis. But it flew and it flew well. Late spring and all summer Jake and Willy would buzz small farm towns of Arkansas and set the plane down in a field. Jake grinned at the way he felt up in that plane, above the trees, houses, towns. The air would blow all around him and he felt free. It was an incredible sensation. He had always wanted to pilot it, but Willy never let him. Jake's job was to go into town on foot and sell! He would drum up business for people to go out and take a 15 minute ride. Back then people were still in awe of those motorized birds in the sky and few had the experience of flying so, even though purses were tight, a ride in a plane was a once in a lifetime chance. The business went well. Grinning his little grin and with a little chuckle (Jake never laughed a hearty laugh, just a chuckle) he remembered how he slept under the plane each night during those summer days protecting Willy's interest. That feeling of freedom and the carefree times of childhood were coming back to him and he decided as he watched those air cadets that his purpose in the United States war effort was to be a pilot.

Thank goodness Jake had the perfect acquaintance to help make it happen, the Navy Chief, his friend. The chief came back to Jake with the answers he had asked him about,

"How do I become one of them?" as he pointed to the cadets. He had to qualify, of course. Senior officers (active and retired) who had served with Jake in his various assignments, readily vouched for his proficiency, attention to duty and excellent record so he had a chance to at least apply to be a Naval pilot. An appointment was arranged for him to try to qualify for the flight training program. At the time, only cadets with at least two years of college were accepted, however, under the Navy's V-5 Program he could qualify for the program as a high school graduate, providing he could pass the qualifying exams; both physical and mental. That was not a problem. He passed with flying colors and the Navy requested that USMC Commandant honorably discharge Platoon Sergeant Nelson Edward Jacobs from the USMC so he could be enlisted into the Navy V-5 Program and begin his Navy's preflight school at the University of Georgia, Athens, Georgia immediately as a lone Joint Program member. He was the one and only one of these at that time. His Honorable Discharge from USMC came on July 23, 1942 and he was enlisted into the Navy Reserve from July 24, 1942 until August 6, 1942. If all went well he would become a naval flight cadet.

Never a student per se, Jake studied harder than ever before. The more he studied, the more he was intrigued with school and all the knowledge it can give a person. Interesting how throughout the years of school, boys fight so hard to be free from it only to realize later on that school offers not only opportunities, but learning can be inspirational and healthy. That is called maturity. And Jake was getting it. Assigned to a platoon in Georgia he was on his first leg of a long, hard year of difficult work. He attended classes at the University of Georgia. Math classes were his most challenging and on most Saturdays he had to go to "dumb" school. These were the makeup sessions for math for the students who could not "get it" the first time. Eventually he managed to graduate in spite of math and was on his way to Navy Primary Flight School in St. Louis, Missouri via a short stopover in Washington, D.C. to visit with his long time friends and colleagues at the Navy Yard.

He jumped an Air Force transport to Lambert Field at the St. Louis Naval Air Station. It became a Naval Air Reserve facility during World War II as an active-duty installation. Excitement filled Jake's bones. This was it. He had the chance of a lifetime to become a pilot and he was not going to miss it. He had worked hard for it so far, and he was determined to succeed. The United States needed him. He needed to prove to himself that he could do it. He had no one at home waiting for him so he was free; free to become who he was destined to be.

He was assigned an instructor at the Navy Flight Office at Pulford on August 7, 1942. He was now enlisted as a U.S. Naval Reserve Aviation Cadet. As soon as he was issued his uniform and equipment he was ready to commence flight training. It was a seven days a week program including both day and night training. Not only was he learning to fly but the entire purpose was military flying which meant training in cross country dive bombing, flying-over exercises with both aerial and ground targets over water, navigation and aircraft maintenance. The planes were not like the Spirit of St. Louis, they were military planes all of which he was required to be proficient at flying. Included in these planes were most importantly the North American SNJ-4 Texan (Scout trainer) with one engine, a range of 750 miles and a maximum speed of 205 mph, , the SBD-5 Douglas Dauntless dive bomber single engine with a 1,115 miles range, maximum speed of 255mph, and the Curtiss SB2C Helldiver, single engine dive bomber with range of 1,165 miles, maximum speed of 295 mph. Flight training exercises also included operations and intelligence. No wonder he needed some college courses. Alertness, a sense of calm, diligence. All these qualities that Jake had acquired in the marines could save his life as well as others. Jake was energized by his flight training and knew he had chosen the right path. Going up and down in the sky at high speeds certainly gave him satisfaction. It was an incredible and unforgettable experience for the Arkansas fellow who loved barnstorming and had never grown sea legs during his U.S.S. Chaumont days!

    He was discharged as a U.S. Naval Reserve Aviation Cadet on July 5, 1943, just in time for World War II to be really heating up. The United States needed more dive bomb pilots to win the war in the Pacific. Needed them and had to have them trained quickly and well. With his new enlistment to the U. S. Marine Corps Reserve as Second Lieutenant on July 6, 1943, Jake began his active duty and more dive bomb training at Pensacola, Florida at the Naval Air Training

Center. Completing three months of intense advance training in simulated combat, dive bombing and flying patrols on the East coast of Florida and adjacent islands, Jake and the other air cadets were continually patrolling along the East coast which included scouting missions. Cadets were used because the fully trained dive bombers were already in the Pacific actively going head to head with the enemies of our country, the Japanese. The next stop for training was the West coast; the land of his dreams. Beautiful coastline, the Pacific Ocean and beautiful women. Off to California. Once again, Jake felt life was going his way as an officer, a pilot and an American.

Chapter 6: California Here I Come...

Immediate reporting for aviation duty was ordered for Second Lieutenant Nelson Edward Jacobs, USMCR (NAVC). No dilly dallying around. No short leaves to visit with anyone; he had no one to go visit anyway. He was to proceed overland to the Marine Corps Aviation Base, Kearney Mesa, San Diego, California and report to the Commanding General with the Marine Aircraft Wings, Pacific. He reported before midnight as ordered. His five day trip on the bus was a time for Jake to contemplate. He thought about how fast his life was moving; Pearl Harbor attack, re-upping in the Marine Corps, becoming a Naval Air Cadet, pilot training. He had no real time to think about his personal life until this long bus trip across the United States. As he watched the varying landscapes of our great country stream past him, his mind could not help but to ponder about his love life. Of course, that was diminished by the "Dear John" letter in China, but now as America's scenery whizzed past him, he was actually grateful he had no ties. Past bitterness over a relationship would not help him at all. He could concentrate on doing what he had to do; protect our homeland and bomb the hell out of the Japs! Personal relationships could wait until the war was over, or so he thought!

Jake's assignment on the West Coast was at the Marine Corps Air Station, El Toro, California. El Toro was seven miles from the town of Santa Ana, Orange County near

Los Angeles. Once the 107,000 acre Irvine Ranch that the Navy purchased for a blimp base, El Toro became a Marine Air Station after Pearl Harbor to provide antisubmarine patrols for the Los Angeles harbor. In July 1943 the base began the mission of training replacement pilot and crews. The losses of existing squadrons in the Pacific were becoming astronomical and new personnel were needed quickly. By March 1944 El Toro became almost entirely a training center for fighter and scout-bomber replacement pilots. The Curtiss SB2C Helldiver, (Jake's preferred dive bomber) was acquired from the British because it was not their preferred dive bomber. Because the U.S. quickly needed more dive bombers, The Navy purchased and took them out of the Brits' hands and they were delivered to El Toro, bringing aircraft there to 237.

Once checking in with the proper authorities and the fancy paperwork by the U. S. Government was completed, Jake joyfully caught a ride to Santa Ana, California breathing the fresh California air, watching the crashing waves of the Pacific, and feeling proud he would be one of the protectors of this great land called America. Upon arriving at El Toro Air Base, he was assigned to the 132nd Marine Scout Bombing Squadron (VMSB 132), commanded by Lt. Col. Calhoun. Assigned to his "new temporary home", he met Lt. Stubby Nelson, a native of Taos, New Mexico. Stubby got his name from his short height. The two roommates became fast friends. Also among the aviators at El Toro was John Glenn, awaiting his final orders to the Marshall Islands. Although Glenn was not at El Toro long, Jake and he shared a beer or two telling tales from home and training experiences. Jake found him to be a really nice guy from Ohio, but not such a good pilot. Since Glenn was a F4U Corsair fighter pilot, Jake figured he didn't need to have the skills of the dive bomb pilot; just lots of guts! The VMSB 132 was on alert 24 hours daily. This was not "just" training, it was active duty too! Excitement and energy was always a force to deal with. Day and night. There was very little down time. Every "t" was crossed and every "I" was dotted to insure that every pilot was trained by the book. But, sometimes that was not enough. There were still accidents; deadly accidents. Twice during the next few months Jake was assigned the somber duty of notifying next to kin of pilots killed during training exercises. When these horrific accidents happened, location of the pilots' remains was not an easy task. Sobering as these deaths were, each Marine knew it could happen to him. Each understood the dangers. Jake was determined to be diligent, attentive at all times, to live! His number had not yet come up. He silently hoped Lady Luck would stay on his side.

Chapter 7: The Red-Headed Firecracker

The little down time Jake had during the intensive pilot training and missions at El Toro, was spent in Santa Monica, California. After a pleasant, calming 15 mile open air street car ride, it was a place he found to be totally relaxing; a place he could calm his nerves and enjoy the Pacific coastline and the tall palm trees swaying in the breeze as well as the beautiful California women. Many times Jake and a couple of his officer buddies would spend a few hours in Los Angeles at the Brown Derby, a lively dining and bar hangout with live music. It was located on Wilshire Blvd. just across from the well known Ambassador Hotel. As fun as that was, sometimes Jake relished an evening out alone. Jake was not a womanizer by any means. He was handsome with a serious but kind demeanor. He was soft spoken, had a charming grin, Southern boy manners. Certainly, a man that could attract a woman; and the Marine officer uniform didn't hurt either. Use all the tools available to you, right? One such excursion Jake found himself at the top notch Hotel Miramar bar minding his own business, watching the attractive crowd, and sipping a cold beer. Jake enjoyed this particular bar in lieu of the local lower class beach bars that enticed most of the service men. Having been raised in an upper class, highly educated family from Arkansas, he didn't mind spending extra for a beer now and then at an upper crust bar! And, oh, the ladies in this bar! Dressed to the nines. He liked that. He respected a well spoken, well dressed woman. They were much more enjoyable to talk to than the fun loving, wildly flirtatious girls at the beach bars.

As he was once again contemplating his duties at El Toro, he was silently sipping his beer, hoping to let down and relax so he could get his mind off his job. He was just finishing his first beer when a fantastically elegant woman sat down in the bar stool next to him. Later he could not remember what he noticed first; the auburn hair, the steamy blue eyes, the radiant smile, the long legs with those red high heels, the perfume, or her engaging voice. He was stunned. He could only look at her and smile. He felt himself lucky he had just swallowed the last sip of that beer, for surely he would have spit it out by the nearness to this woman. She began the introductions and before he knew it, he felt he had known her forever. This wonderful woman's name was Virginia Lea, born in Oakland, California, raised mostly in Pasadena. She came from quite a well to do family, "not aristocratic" she explained to Jake. As Jake ordered another beer for himself and a Martini for Virginia, he learned more. As she spoke, he realized he also was sharing his history. Although each claimed they were not Aristocrats by any means, they each had colored servants in their homes as they were growing up. No one dug things out of him as well as she did. She got him joining in the conversation as though Jake talked all the time. Wow! What a feat.

Virginia had been a Rose Parade Princess in Pasadena in 1937. She was accustomed to people paying attention to her, drew attention everywhere she went, as he would soon find out. Her mother, she said, was a force to be reckoned with and she had a younger sister who was her complete opposite. Virginia was well-educated, in fact, she had tutored Jackie Robinson at Pasadena Community College and helped him to be accepted into UCLA. She showed absolute tolerance for others; she loved all people no matter what color they were. Having served in the military for five plus years by now, Jake agreed with her. He had served with all colors in the USMC and been exposed to many different cultures in his military travels. He admired her way of thinking and her energy. She certainly was her own woman and so attractive in every way: physically and academically. And she was a firecracker, in a good way! Oh, boy. Jake was beginning to feel his being free to not worry about having emotional ties just might be fading. He was right!

As Jake rode the "red" line street car back to El Toro late that night, he could not stop feeling the excitement about his future was coming alive again. All because of this frisky female he met. They had made plans to meet at the Hotel Miramar the next week. He had her phone number so he could call her if his schedule was unexpectedly changed by the Marine Corps. The next Wednesday at 5 p.m. he could once again be enchanted by this California woman. Lucky guy!

Chapter 8: The War and Romance Heat Up

As the war heated up in both the Pacific and European theaters, Jake and his squadron worked longer hours. Scouting the coastline was 24/7 and training exercises were continuous. Although Jake anxiously anticipated his meeting with Virginia, he could not ignore or neglect his wartime duties. As a pilot of the British made Curtiss SB2C Helldiver, he became more proficient at dropping bombs on his targets with accuracy. It was widely agreed upon by the USMCR and Navy pilots that the replacement of the Douglas SBD Dauntless, the Curtiss SB2C Helldiver was not as well liked. However, the new diver was able to attack with higher precision on naval and land targets, it was faster than the Dauntless, it had tricolor camouflage on its undersides, plus the cockpit was redesigned to give both the pilot and his gunner a better view. However, the first Helldivers used in El Toro during the war had unreliable electrical systems. Another major problem with them was the range of a fully bomb loaded Helldiver was not as long as the Dauntless and that ended with 45 Helldivers being lost during the Battle of the Philippines' Sea because they ran out of fuel before they could return to their aircraft carriers. As it turned out, the Curtiss SB2C and Dauntless dive bombers went on to sink more ship tonnage than any other aircraft in World War II.

Even knowing the inefficiency of his wartime plane, everything about piloting a dive bomber excited Jake; the

90 degree climb and then the 70 degree dive, and then the abrupt pull-up after dropping the bomb. It was a rush; more so than the scouting missions. But, he was not in battle, yet!

Jake and his gunner, W. W. King became trustworthy flying partners and good friends. The relationship with your gunner was vital for survival. As the pilot of the Helldiver controlled the altitude, climbs, and bombs, the gunner navigated, was in control of the radio, and protected the dive bomber by being proficient at using the two mounted 7.62mm M1919 Browning air-cooled machine guns in the rear cockpit. The pilot had control of the fixed forward-firing 20 mm cannons in the wings, the internal bay which held 2,000 pounds of bombs or one torpedo and the under wing 500 pound bombs. The Helldiver was 10,547 pounds empty; loaded it was extremely heavy. Although Jake had trained on taking off and landing on an aircraft carrier, he was happy not to be stationed on one. Many a dive bomber had ended up in the drink (Ocean) because of a bad takeoff or landing. Scariest part of flying he had experienced yet was the aircraft carrier training. And that was with no bombs on his plane. So many times at night when Jake fell dead tired into his bunk in the officer quarters, he had gone to sleep thankful he was not in the "hot" areas. He had a sinking feeling during the week after meeting Virginia that his time was coming; he just prayed it was not before he saw her again.

Finally, Wednesday arrived and the "red" street car seemed to crawl at a record slow pace to Santa Monica. Jake's feet hit the pavement before the trolley came to a stop and he was at the Hotel Miramar bar just three minutes before his firecracker appeared looking as fresh as a rose! She brightened the dark paneled bar with the heavy velvet drapes as she gracefully promenaded her way to him. Once again Jake could not believe this angel, Virginia, wanted to be with him! He stood up to welcome her and pulled the stool out for her. As she daintily sat down, he quivered as her red dress showed some of her leg. Breathless, after a drink each, they entered the dining room of the Miramar; white table clothes, red roses adorning each table, crystal, china, expensive! Jake knew it would cost him his week's pay or maybe more, but it was worth it! They ate, drank, talked, fell in love! Each was mesmerized by the other.

The romance continued as Jake continued to take every spare moment he could muster up to be with her. He began calling her Dixie; a nickname she had received well before he knew her. They danced to the music of Tommy Dorsey and Bing Crosby. Thank goodness Jake was athletic for he had never danced before; Dixie was patient and loved to dance! Once he got the hang of the "swing", he was unstoppable. One of their favorite places for a good show and dancing was the Copacabana in Long Beach. When he had an afternoon free, Jake would jump the "red" street car and join Dixie for a ride on the Looft Hippodrome, the famous Merry-Go-Round on Santa Monica Pier. They had full control of the street cars for transportation and fortunately, Dixie who worked for B.F. Goodrich, helped pay for many of their drinks although Jake did not like that. It was not how things should be. Men paid for everything. It was a matter of honor. But once Dixie had something in her head, there was no use trying to stop her. He began to understand that, many times to his chagrin, but he had great respect for this out-spoken, articulate and fun woman. She was in charge and Jake was having the time of his life.

He met Dorothy, her mother. He immediately realized from whom Dixie had learned to be independent. Both were beautiful and strong-willed females. Dorothy made Jake feel like he was part of the family and he began to meet them in the mountains just outside of Los Angeles in a very small community called Green Valley Lake. It was so peaceful there. Dorothy had inherited some money from her family in Chicago and wanted to build a cabin so Jake immediately volunteered his services thus securing a better footing in his relationship with Dixie's family. When he could not be there on the weekends to build, he flew over during his scouting flights and tipped his wings. That would clinch the seal of approval from Dorothy for her daughter's choice in a man. As their relationship blossomed, so did his concern of going to the Pacific.

Chapter 9: Oops!

VMSB was placed on alert! It was the fall of 1944 and training flights were more demanding. The pilots had no idea that was possible; except in the actual combat. Two fellow pilots and their gunners were killed during this period of training. Every military personnel took this hard. What a waste! Jake resolved once again to be alert, exact, and smart.

Duke was on a training mission one Sunday morning and found his aircraft enveloped in a solid fog a mile over water. He had flown from the surface to about 10,000 feet altitude, flying wide and was forced to make short turns to avoid a sharp move so as not to strain his engines. Visibility was zero and there was no horizon to fix upon. Sometimes the horizon and the water becomes one to a pilot flying over the ocean; very dangerous! The plane had lost altitude but Jake did not know how much, he could only estimate how many feet he was flying from the ocean's surface. W.W. King, the gunner, was attempting to jump, but they were too low to safely jump. King, the gunner yelled in his mike, "Let's get out of here." They did! Shaking like a leaf, Jake managed to avoid the water, brought the plane to a safer altitude and headed back to El Toro barely managing to safely land at the last second. A near miss. Jake got permission to take the following day off.

Several days later, the war temperature spiraled up again with intelligence briefings increasing with the mid-

Pacific seeming to be the focal point of the war in the Pacific. In addition, flights to local target areas were never ending. One favorite auxiliary airfield was at Clark Dry Lake area, about 50 miles east of El Toro.

A squadron briefing produced the announcement that the entire squadron would attack the Clark Dry Lake Auxiliary Airfield. Take-off time was 0545 the next morning. Jake and Gunner King huddled and went over all equipment on the Curtiss SB3C they were scheduled to fly. Next morning at 0600, Jake started to his plane but did not see W.W. King anywhere. Another gunner approached him with the news that King would not be making the flight with Jake, but with the Commanding Officer to Mole Square Field for deck landing exercises. "Lieutenant, you fly solo today; here are your instructions." Jake quickly opened and read, "Approach Clark Dry Lake target from the west at 13,000 feet- one approach to target, make drop and return to base." The entire squadron made their approved course, led by the Commanding Officer. As Jake was rolling his plane over to sight his target, dead silence! No noise from the engine. He first checked the fuel gages; all indicated ample fuel. Then he went through all the failed engine procedures; nothing! Oops! Might be why the Brits didn't like this Curtiss so much! Every effort failed so he nosed over slightly and looked for a crash landing site below. He looked for other squadron members since Jake had pulled out of the formation. None!

Jake never liked to jump off high things; not diving boards, not cliffs and certainly not out of a plane. That was the reason he decided not to eject when his dive bomber malfunctioned. The choice to Jake was simple; stay with the plane and take his chances on crashing. As his dive bomber lost altitude it came closer to the inevitable crash, he braced himself and tried to dismiss the memories racing through his mind. After all, isn't that what happens when you are experiencing a near death episode? The emotional pain and regret of his girlfriend in Arkansas who he left behind six years earlier kept flashing through his mind. The guilt, the longing; and then, the incredibly engaging blue eyed and red headed firecracker that was waiting for him in California. No matter! He was not ejecting...

As he wandered away from the crash site, he was amazed at still being alive and congratulated himself for not bailing! A near miss. As was Jake's way, his brain switched from his near death memories to the problems at hand. Was he going to get court marshaled for crashing the million dollar U.S. Navy government issued Curtiss SB2C Helldiver? In the middle of nowhere, with severe shock setting in, he tried to concentrate on staying alive. One way was to get away from the Helldiver, after all, it was full of gas and could explode any second. But what was that rattling sound? And flying sand? Sounded like shooting and bullets hitting.....a couple days later 10,000 bullet cases were counted in the exact area of where Second Lieutenant Nelson E. Jacobs crashed his bomber.

Although a bit in shock, he realized that live fire rounds were the reason for the rattling sounds. It was friendly fire; a

National Guard unit from Indiana was out on desert training exercises. The guardsmen were in a line of jeeps firing into the area Jake just happened to be. The last jeep carried the Sergeant of the unit who glanced up and notice movement up the hill from him. What was that, an animal? With binoculars posed, he realized it was a man! It was Jake! He ran to him, identified himself with Jake informing him that he had been on a dive-bomb exercise and his engine quit, thus crashing! Jake told he was from UMSB 132 at El Toro, California and asked the Sergeant to please inform them he was okay. However, he knew his plane was not! After Jake's superior officer was informed, he was taken to spend the night with the Guardsmen since it was growing dark. What Jake did not know was that he was being watched for injuries due to his crash landing and his disorientation. By morning, he was fit to find his way to the Naval Training field not far away from where he had spent the night. Saying his thanks to his finders, he was being taken by jeep down the road to the Naval Training field when they came upon a small convoy carrying his crashed plane, loaded on a lowboy truck. At that moment Jake felt the Navy cared more about wrecked aircrafts than they did about their pilots. His dive bomber would reach El Toro before him! However, a short time later, the guardsman turned into a small airstrip and quickly dropped Jake off in front of a small metal building. He was offered a folding cot for the night and rations for nourishment with the promise to be picked up from someone out of El Toro the next day. An older gentleman appeared known by the Airmen in charge of the airstrip. He appeared to know all about Jake's problem and said, "I live just a bit from here and have a spare bed in my place. How 'bout sleepin' on a bed until your friends pick you up? I have a phone and you can be reached anytime." With a senior officer's approval, Jake thankfully climbed into the old guy's truck and was driven to an older home, chowed-down on a home cooked meal, and soon fell asleep on a clean comfortable bed. Jake had defied death 10,002 times. One of the 10,000 bullets could have killed him. The crash could have killed him. If not spotted by the Sergeant of the last jeep, the shock and outdoor elements could have killed him. 10,002 near misses!

The phone did not ring until the following day with a pick up from El Toro. Finally, at dusk, of the third day, a small U.S. Navy plane landed and a pilot announced, "Jacobs! I'm here to return you to El Toro." An hour and a half later Duke was in the 'Ready' room of VMSP 132 being debriefed. "Yup", thought Jake, "They definitely care more about a dive bomber than the pilot." Although Jake knew how the military was, it was reality at that moment to him; it seemed it should be the Marine first, the plane next! Ah well. He was alive and ready to continue his duties. Why stress? After all, he had Dixie! But, Dixie would have to wait for on the following day he was briefed by the squadron intelligence officer that his squadron was being deactivated and about ready to move within the next 48 hours. He was advised that he would be joining Major Ayres and others at the Naval Air Station in Hawaii. There, his group would receive instructions for proceeding to an unnamed destination in the Marshall Islands reporting in to squadron VMSB 245. Jake hurriedly collected his personal belongings and flight gear, vacated his quarters, said goodbye to his roommates and phoned Dixie, caught the 'red' line to Santa Monica, bought a last minute item, and met his red-headed firecracker one hour later at the Hotel Miramar.

As brave as a love sick Marine could be, he told Dixie of his orders to the Pacific. Being a well informed young woman, she knew that was the area of the Pacific that was the most dangerous. The Japanese were, with deadly force, taking control of one small island at a time leaving massive carnage of American military men and planes. The young couple knew this could be the last time they would be together, but neither could even hint it…for that thought broke both of their hearts! As Jake and Dixie strolled along the ocean walk by the hotel, Jake went down on one knee, dug deep into his pocket and took out a small jewelry box. "Will you marry me, Virginia Lea?" With tears in her eyes and love in her heart she replied, "Of course." As Jake slipped the diamond ring onto her finger, he thought, I have a ring on her finger and now she is mine! No worries. Someone to come home to!

As they were saying their goodbyes, Virginia reached into her purse and brought out a small pocket Bible. As she gave it to Jake, she made him promise to keep it with him at all times and to use it! "Never hurts to pray and be reminded of my mortality," thought Jake. Sadly, they departed company as Jake caught a government bus to San Diego to catch the transport ready to sail. Six days later, in November of 1944, the ship docked and the Marine pilots were directed to the Hawaiian Naval Air Station to make ready to depart to their ultimate destination, the Marshall Islands.

Chapter 10: The Real Deal

As the Marine pilots and gunners approached Pearl Harbor they were shocked at the horrific damage to the ships, planes, and base that the Japs had wreaked. Jake choked back tears as he led his squadron to the barracks. How could so much damage be done by such a small, but obviously mean, country? The attack on Pearl Harbor on December 7, 1941 by the Imperial Japanese Navy, killed 2403 Americans and wounded 1178. Along with that, three cruisers, three destroyers, 188 U.S. aircraft were all destroyed. Simultaneously, the Japanese were also invading the Philippines, Guam and Wake Island in one coordinated surprise plot to prevent the United States and their allies from interfering in their accumulation of Southeast Asia. By 1937 the Japanese were expanding their control of China as Jake had already seen. The mastermind behind the attacks was Tojo Hideki who had dictatorial control of Japan. What the Japanese did not count on was our retaliation; they assumed the United States would negotiate resources with them, not declare war since the United States was already at war with Germany and the Axis Powers. Surely the United States did not have the resources for two wars. The dictator of Japan, Tojo, was wrong. The Americans were furious and so was the government. On December 8, 1941 President Roosevelt declared war on Japan. On December 9, 1941 Jake re-enlisted into the Marines with the company of thousands of other American men who enlisted into the military to fight not just Hitler, but Tojo!

The Japanese military had no idea the strength of the "angry tiger" they had released. The Battle of Midway was planned six months after Pearl Harbor was attacked. Thanks to the Japanese code being broken, the US Military formed a plan to payback what the Japs had done to them on that "Day in infamy." Just as the Japs had surprised America, the U.S. military paid a surprise visit to the enemy. With scout planes finding the Japanese fleet and aircraft, torpedo bombers and dive bombers attacked with full force. Tragically, 36 out of the 42 torpedo bombers were lost but they had diverted the Japanese long enough for the dive bombers to arrive and make havoc on the enemy. It cost 300 American lives and 147 aircraft, however, the victory allowed the United States and its allies to move into an offensive position for the rest of the war.

The Battle of Okinawa began on March of 1945 and ended June 22, 1945 killing 14,000 U.S. Army men, Navy deaths totaled 4,907 including Marine pilots and gunners, and 763 U.S. aircraft were lost. It was vital to keep control of Okinawa because in order to invade the Island of Japan, the U.S. and its allies would have to have their airbases located in Okinawa. As the Japanese attacked over and over, the Allied forces faced their most difficult Pacific campaign. What the Allied forces did not realize was the drop of morale in the ranks of Japanese pilots although that did not diminish the enemy pilot's determination to do their duty to death. Kamikaze pilots planned to die which made them even more dangerous.

Unlike the American pilots, the Japanese had orders to not rescue downed planes because that would distract from their job; win the war! Loss of compassion for others made them even deadlier!

Just knowing the recent history of the Pacific war, Jake would sometimes wake up at night sweating. He was not a worrier, he was a doer; even so, the stories and truths of the fight in the Pacific were terrifying! Even the best pilots had been killed, captured or eaten by sharks. Actually, Jake could not decide which would be worse; killed, eaten or captured. The Japanese did not follow the Geneva Convention agreement that followed World War I: they did what they wanted to their prisoners of war

As the Battle of Okinawa was raging, Jake spent just a couple weeks in Hawaii going on scouting missions and dive bomb practices. Finally, he got his orders to board a U.S. military transport aircraft and report in at the Island of Majuro Atoll, one of the Marshall islands that gave the U.S. Navy the use of one of the largest anchorages in the Central Pacific and most active port until the war moved westward when it was replaced by Ulithi Atoll. But as the transport plane from Hawaii left Jake and his squadron at this small island in the Pacific, Jake focused day and night on surviving and winning the war for every American, but especially for Dixie. A couple days later, the transport ship arrived with the planes. As each pilot checked out his plane, many painted a name or a picture on his own. Some painted artistically voluptuous women but for Jake he just wrote: DIXIE! Yes, he had a plane named Dixie and nothing and nobody would hurt her, he hoped!

Upon arrival to the small island, the incoming Marines learned that their squadron had the responsibility of maintaining surveillance over some of the by-passed Japanese islands. This could have been a problem if the Japanese had been left to their own devices; for example, refueling their submarines and aircraft for additional attacks within the U.S. area of operation and thus enabling them to have access to the U.S. fleet and shore installations. To deny them of this advantage, the squadron immediately began bombing and strafing the islands of Mille, Jalui, Wotje, Malolap and other islands located in the Marshall Islands chain. This included flying patrols almost 24 hours daily to insure that the Japanese were not able to re-enforce or resupply these strategic, but by passed, bases.

One of the most devastating disasters during Jake's participation in the Pacific War came one Saturday evening. As the leader of the squadron and one of the older and more experienced Marine pilots, Jake was responsible for behavior of his men; on and off duty! Every one needed a break now and then and booze was available during those times. A senior officer could do just so much to monitor behaviors as was apparent that fateful Saturday night. Jake awoke to planes in the air; he quickly threw on his battle gear and ran to the airstrip, ready to take off in "Dixie" to avenge the attackers. There were no attackers, only two young pilots from his squadron already in the air at 2 in the morning.

They were making loops and thinking they were performing at an air show. With great fear, Jake realized he had seen the two at the base's club just a couple hours before. They were drunk apparently for who would be so stupid to be doing circus acts with SB2C dive bombers if they weren't. There was no way to contact them since they did not have gunners with them; thank God for that! As they were trying to coordinate a synonymous loop, they hit each other head on....the explosion, the fire, no ejections. Both pilots were killed and both planes were lost! Jake was sickened. He would be the one to write the report, shoulder the guilt and responsibility, write the letters home. As many tragic and inhumane incidents Jake would see during that war, that one disaster stayed with him, forever.

In addition to the normal assignment of flight missions, Jake and his gunner were ordered to the Eniwietok Atoll to participate in joint navy-marine anti-submarine warfare exercises. Of course, Jake was wondering why he had to play war games when they actually had war flaring all around, but he was not one to question his senior officer or the Marines. The exercises included changing duty assignments with the submariners. This meant the pilots took the duties of a submarine officer and a submarine officer took over the duties of an airplane gunner, thus giving each other a feel for the other duties and responsibilities. When it came his turn to become a member of a submarine crew and to practice evasive actions to avoid the airplanes, Jake was not the most enthusiastic Marine pilot around. But, being macho Marines,

Jake went as ordered Then and there Jake decided that the life of a submariner was not for him. No siree! After Jake and his pseudo gunner, a submarine officer, steamed out into the open sea, they made a total of eight dives with their own planes dropping dummy depth charges on them when they thought that they had located and identified the submarine as the enemy. After landing, Jake noticed the ashen color of the pseudo gunner's and realized he was happy to go back to his duty on the ship. Jake walked away with a great deal of admiration for the submariners. When the exercise was completed they flew back to Majuro only to find that the squadron was being relocated to Ulithi in the Caroline Islands. The orders were the same – protect the fleet. Almost everyone except some of the pilots and other key personnel went by Navy sea transport; Jake was flown in a Marine transport plane about 1,000 miles to their destination.

Taken over by the U.S. Navy in September of 1944, Ulithi Atoll, a small chain of three dozen choral islands located in the Caroline Islands, had been just recently abandoned by the Japanese who used it for a radio and weather station. Once the US Navy transferred the local islanders to the another island for the duration of the war, the Navy built Ulithi Atoll into a complete floating base with 6,000 ship fitters, artificers, welders, carpenters and electricians to repair ships, destroyer tenders and floating dry docks. The lagoon could hold up to 700 vessels. There were also fleet oilers which refueled the warships a short distance from their combat operational areas. An airstrip was constructed on Falatop, one of the islands. Ulithi Atoll serviced the military operations for the entire Pacific fleet, some of which were a couple thousand miles away. This enabled the U.S. to sustain operations in the Western Pacific without returning to the Naval base at Pearl Harbor. Ulithi Atoll, 360 miles SW of Guam and 1300 miles South of Tokyo, was an unknown base to the American public and to the Japanese who had no idea that it had become the largest U. S. Naval base during World War II.

Just a couple weeks before Jake's squadron's arrival at the Caroline Islands, in November of 1944, the Ulithi Atoll harbor was attacked by the Japanese destroying the fleet oiler, USS Mississinewa. Unfortunately, that was not the last attack on Ulithi Atoll. Jake would have first-hand experience scouting missions that would help to avoid many more attempts by the Japanese to take control of the Caroline Islands.

Among the key personnel on the Marine air transport plane to Uilthi was Sgt. Land, a retired Washington, D.C. policeman who was to work with and became fast friends with Jake in getting the new camp organized and set up since the 245 was to Island Hop from that location using the small recently completed airstrip. Jake saw the 3200 foot runway and he almost fainted. No planes had yet landed on it and he wondered who would be the first; a Marine or Navy plane. It would be a couple of weeks before they would find out since there was so much to do to make this tiny island their home. Since the only useable item on the island was the airstrip that the Seabees had just completed, the two pals approached the supply personnel of the Seabees, the Port Captain. They figured he could either come up with some items himself or know how to get them. They were able to get enough tents to put together a make shift camp until they could make further improvements. Through perseverance, hard work, and ingenuity Jake and the sergeant managed to make their island of Falatop the best military area in the Pacific; or so they personally thought! And, of course, a Marine plane was the first to land on the airstrip! They even ended up with a 24 hour snack bar. The principle way of obtaining items that they needed or thought they needed was to have volunteers work for the navy whenever they needed manpower. That way the men always came back with something needed and the Navy got free labor, almost. They were able to keep their snack bar well stocked with all sorts of goodies. With the lumber they were able to get by bartering, they were able to put flooring in all the tents for the men. They never did get wood for the officers' tents except for the Commanding Officer. It paid off to have all the men as happy as a person could make them, especially since they were all risking their lives for their country, including the CO. The Navy base was so well supplied that there was even a US vessel that made 500 gallons of ice cream a day! The United States truly knew how to keep morale among the troops up and one of the troops, Jake, loved ice cream! He was in charge of making sure his squadron received at least their fair portion of it; just like the freshly baked bread on the ship to China, Jake positioned himself to always be able to enjoy his favorite treat on this island that was only a pencil point on every world map. Jake enjoyed his part in the organization and building of a community and he wrote Dixie telling her all about it. As he wrote he thought she would certainly understand this kind of emotional work for she was a very giving, energetic person who respected this kind of effort. He sent the letter praying he would still be alive by the time she received it.

A new community of men and the teambuilding they encouraged helped to deal with living on an island with high humidity, thick tropical forests, and insects never seen before. The military had to brave dangers of combat as well as disease. Jake and his fellow marines were briefed on these dangers along with the everyday reminder that being captured by the cruel enemy, ejecting from a plane into the flimsy lifeboat with sharks surrounding it, a deadly crash into the ocean, or being shot down were all very real possibilities. Somehow the new insects and high humidity was nothing! Just do your job! Be a Marine!

Finally, the dive bombers had been delivered to the atoll and each pilot and gunner began patrolling immediately. Jake's first flight from the new, mud packed airstrip was on March 31, 1945. The lagoon was now filling up with ships and the navy was insistent that they provide air cover full time. Not even the weather prevented patrols from going out, and as Jake learned, the tropical winds and rains were something to reckon with as a pilot. In addition to patrolling, they had to maintain close surveillance over the Island of Yap which was located 103 miles away and still occupied by the

Japanese. This was a major threat to the US fleet because of the refueling capability they still had on the by-passed islands. Therefore, Jake bombed and strafed that island at least three times a week. Sometimes he went alone, and if intelligence had an indication that something was unusual taking place the entire squadron would bomb Yap. Jake did not feel it was usually very exciting, since it was simply drop the bombs and go back and land, but it was necessary. During the summer of 1945, the purge in the Pacific was on. Air strikes, antisubmarine patrols and missions to Guam for replacement planes and parts were critical for each mission. More and more Navy ships were departing from the busy base and more protective missions were flown. In June one strike ended in the loss of one of UMSB 245's plane and crew. Jake assisted in the rescue of survivors of the downed plane by circling the airplane for several hours, pin-pointing survivors until a Navy crew rescued them. There were no losses of life. July and August drug on, but not without some horrific moments for the dive bombers and their crews. Jake was thankful for the newer SB2C's higher altitude capacity and the bullet proof metal backed seats. Not just once, but several times, he was coming down from his dive to drop his load of bombs on Yap, when King spotted Zeros in range. Jake figured the Japs were getting a little tired of bombs being dropped on one of the islands they still had control of. Unfortunately, these were the times he had made solo flights, without the squadron. Why not easily pick one off at a time, right? One dive bomber is an easy target, so they thought! With the improved windows of the Curtiss SB2C, Jake and King were easily able to see and shoot down the attackers. However, Jake preferred to be the one coming down from the high altitude on top of a Zero. That way he was on the offence, not the defense and could easily shoot at it to scare it off or have it plunge into the ocean. Each time he encountered a Zero, he shakily went back to the base, checked in to the Galley and had a shot of bourbon, just to settle his nerves. Flying was a rush; shooting down planes and ending a life, was not!

On one such mission, a Zero was quite persistent about its attacks on Jake's plane "Dixie". With bullet holes in the plane, continuous defensive machine gun fire from her heavy equipment on board, and evasive piloting moves from Jake, King ran out of ammunition and decided to throw a grenade from his back seated position. As Jake saw him hurl the grenade, he quickly manipulated "Dixie" to avoid the backlash of the explosion. Either the Zero's suicidal Japanese pilot decided the stupid Americans had blown up their own plane or he decided the American's were crazy, he had retreated by the time "Dixie" recovered. Jake was not happy with his gunner and felt fortunate he had time to get back to base and land before he got his hands on King. Thank God for King that Jake was a cool headed First Lieutenant who knew how to control his emotions because by the time they were on Uthili's solid ground, Jake did not scream at him or hurt him in any way; he only glared with his hazel eyes and with a stern, but kind, voice explained the physics of throwing a grenade out of a plane! Jake took him to the officer's quarters and they both had a shot of bourbon together; or maybe they had two for they had truly defied death. A near miss!

The battles of the Pacific including the surge from the Ulithi, caused Marine pilots to defy death, disease and brave the dangers of combat or being captured by a remorseless enemy. Many died. Many survived against all odds of this horrific war of the Pacific. Each of them had an equal share in bringing the enemy to the doorstep for the Allies final victory. Jake was one of the lucky ones; his expertise, leadership, self resolve made him a survivor, not to mention the help from the little Bible he always kept in his pocket! A near miss!

August 7, 1945 ended up being Jake's last mission in the Pacific. As he logged out in his flight journal after a 2.8 hour local flight test, he and his squadron received orders to evacuate Uthili immediately. Word had been received that the new American secret weapon, Little Boy had been delivered the day before, August 6, 1945, on the Island of Hiroshima. Short on air transport, by the evening of the 7th, the sea transport full of Marines and their planes was on its way headed west in the Pacific. Two days later, while standing on the deck of the American vessel, on August 9, 1945, he along with several of his squadron saw a bright flash of light and then a mushroom cloud on the horizon; Fat Man had been delivered on Nagasaki. As he and his shipmates watched, the second atomic bombs' glorious sight, they prayed this would end the war. It took the Japanese a couple days, but their prayers came true; Thank God!

During the early summer of 1945, the Americans had captured Okinawa where they could launch an invasion of the mainland of Japan and the islands it controlled. U. S. General Douglas MacArthur was in charge of the invasion which was code-named "Operation Olympic". This invasion was to be in November of 1945 and it was predicted to be the bloodiest seaborne attack of all time losing at least 10 times military personnel than the Normandy invasion. Unfortunately for the Japanese, work on a new destructive weapon out in the New Mexico desert was an option for America. The idea of giving up was something the Japanese could and would not do. It would be better to die, to commit suicide than to surrender. As President Truman comprehended this one true fact, he realized that many more Americans and their Allies would die should the war continue. This sentiment led him to approve the atomic bomb, Little Boy, to be dropped on Hiroshima on August 6, 1945. Even that did not make the Japanese concede. Fat Man, was dropped on Nagasaki on August 9, 1945. On August 10, 1945 Japanese Emperor Hirohito negotiated and accepted the option of peace. Peace had come at last. General Douglas MacArthur received the formal surrender from the Japanese Foreign Minister Mamoru Shigemitsu on the USS Missouri on September 2, 1945. Emperor Hirohito continued his reign Japan until his death in 1989. As for Tojo Hideki, he was tried as a war criminal in 1948 and executed! The war in the Pacific had ended. And American military men were returning home to start the Baby Boom; Jake was one of them.

Chapter 11: Civilian Life

The military swarmed back to the mainland of the United States of America with pride, relief, and with earnest to begin the life they had left behind when the country called for them to save democracy and keep America speaking English and not German or Japanese. Jake was one of the proud Marines who made it back in one piece with a woman waiting for him on the docks of this great country. As Jake disembarked from the sea transport, he tried not to tear up. For after all, he was a Marine. But every one of his men were crying and laughing at the same time. The relief, the gratefulness they all felt was beyond anything one could have imagined. As Jake wiped away his tears, he vowed they would be his last for he had grown up since that 19 year old, disappointed high school football player from Arkansas. He had lived through the most horrific war in history, and he was truly a man at 27 years old and ready to begin his new life. He resolved to learn from the past, but to not relive it. Cherish the good, do not dwell on the bad! This would be his promise to himself for the rest of his life; one he never reneged on. And, to him, the most important thing was to continue Chesty's motto: "Be a model of valor by example and precept". This promise and motto would define Jake, forever.

As promised, Virginia Lea White was waiting on the dock for him in Long Beach, California. Her engagement ring and her smile were brightly shining as he found her on the crowded pier of women, children, and families. There was his true love! As she ran into his open arms, he knew his life was good now! The future was theirs. Whatever that meant.

Thousands of men coming home from the European and the Pacific war were ready to settle down and begin their civilian life. For thousands, that began with a marriage. Marriages were at a record high in 1945 and so was the hope of the American people. The United States of America had been in a total war; the women were working outside the homes to support the war effort, the factories had turned production into wartime needs such as uniforms, boots, weapons, ammunition, transportation, and Victory gardens were grown to help supply food to the nation. Now, at last, America could be normal again.

After waiting the California mandated three days to marry after getting a marriage license, on August 31, 1945, Virginia and Jake were standing in the long line to be wed in Riverside County, California by a military chaplain. Usually Jake did not like lines, certainly not long ones, but this was different. He had his bride on his arm, a smile on his face, and hope in his heart. He had survived the war, had not received a purple heart, and he was ready to be a civilian with a beautiful woman that had loyally waited for him. With only one month left of his active military duty, he would have an honorable discharge, combat pay, and a new job at B. F. Goodrich that Virginia had secured for him because she was the assistant to the president of the company. As they dreamily looked into each others' eyes and said their marriage vows, life was good! With a longer than necessary kiss, they signed their document and drove in Virginia's Plymouth Chrysler to the Ambassador Hotel in Los Angeles where they would stay two nights honeymooning; alone with no worries or cares! Jake was dumb struck by the elegance of the hotel, perhaps because he had just spent years on military airstrips, ending with the desolate, primitive islands in the Pacific. But, the Ambassador Hotel had a reputation for famous and rich cliental and Virginia liked the best places, the best food, the best cars. Jake always felt a tad uncomfortable in such fancy places, but he loved to please his new bride.

Then, off to Hotel Del Coronado on Coronado Island in San Diego for a few more days of making love, basking in the sun, and dreaming of their future together. Once again, Jake enjoyed spoiling Virginia. He also was flabbergasted by the beauty of the hotel itself; dark mahogany wood enveloped the lobby, the gold cage-like elevator that glided up and down from the lobby to the upper floors, the views of the clear blue Pacific Ocean, the pure white paint with the steep red roofs towering above the white sand, the divine food service. Jake noticed how peaceful it was, but having been on patrol for months in the Pacific, he was on edge most of the time. It seemed somehow out of sync not to have military planes and patrol boats out on the horizon 24 hours a day. But, Virginia, with her soft, loving ways reassured him the war was over and America was once again safe because of men like himself. Jake was a lucky man to have a wife like her: beautiful, loving, ambitious, and generous.

Since Jake was still in the U.S. Marine Corps, he reported to the Marine Corps Air Depot Miramar, San Diego 48, California and was told he was assigned no duties, he had completed his service and was free to go where he wished as long as he was back by September 27, 1945 to receive his discharge papers. Thrilled with this freedom, he and Virginia temporarily settled in with her mother, Dorothy, on 9th avenue in Los Angeles. Although a very strong minded woman, she was a nurturing, dedicated mother, wife and friend. She, like her daughter, loved to have parties, go to them, and belonged to charitable organizations. They loved people; all people for neither had a racist bone in their body. Living under the same roof with the two women, Jake began to learn what he had gotten himself into. Being from Arkansas, he was a southern boy with southern manners and ideas; especially in the 1940's he believed a man is the breadwinner and the woman is the keeper of the home. It was beginning to dawn on him, that perhaps, Virginia did not see herself as keeper of the home, but they didn't have their own home yet! They would, as soon as they came back to California from taking her to meet his family in McGhee, Arkansas. The two newlyweds sped off in Virginia's Chrysler towards the Southern United States. Oh, what a difference it makes riding across the United States in a car, not a bus or a train, and to not be going to war. The wonders of the countryside intrigued them both; as they shared the driving, for Virginia loved to drive, they told stories of their youth, their hopes and dreams. A little disturbingly, Jake realized they knew very little about each other and they were not always on the same page for their future. Not one to disrupt a serene experience, he decided to keep it to himself. Everything would work out for the two of them for they loved each other very much! Plus, Jake's attention was beginning to focus on his return to his hometown and seeing his family for the first time since he left in 1937. Although he had contact with his father and siblings through the mail, he had no real feelings of emotional ties. He, like many young men, had broken free and was his own man now. Would his father still be authoritarian? Distant as he had always been? This was the way men were; keep emotions to yourself. Right? Jake was a respected First Lieutenant in the U. S. Marine Corps; a war hero who fought for his country! He could surely handle a couple days with a Southern family, even though it was his own!

During the 1940's the Southern United States was a miserable place to live if you were an African American. Even though the Bill of Rights states that all men have equal rights, it didn't look like it from the streets of the south, including McGhee, Arkansas. Every restaurant, public restroom, drinking fountain, store, government building and even schools, had segregation signs. "No blacks allowed", "Whites only" were plastered everywhere. Virginia, being from the West Coast, could not believe her eyes. Jake, being from the South, was accustomed to seeing and living with these signs from his youth, but even he was appalled at seeing them after serving eight years in the military. How could people be so racist? As Jake drove through this small town of only a few thousand, he tried to calm his bride down. He knew he would soon be introducing her to the Mayor of McGhee, his father. Virginia promised to be proper, but she would not like it, not at all! As they joined his family in the parlor of his childhood home Jake was told about the internment camp for Japanese Americans that was built in McGhee. He was surprised to hear it was the largest one in the country. He had heard that America put people of Japanese heritage into these camps to protect them as well as to protect America. He was not sure how he felt about it; it sounded almost un American, but here he was learning there had been one right where he grew up. The parlor conversation turned to news about the new businesses that had cropped up in the town, boys who left for the war and did not return, the pride the family felt for Jake, and questions about Virginia and her upbringing. They were fascinated by her elegance and beauty, her well educated speech, her friendliness and that she was the Rose Parade princess in 1937 in Pasadena, California. Everyone, even the folks in Arkansas, had heard of that famous parade that boasts sunshine, floats covered with flower petals, and the beautiful people of California. Jake was relieved, his family seemed to be accepting his wife as one of their own. Why not go out and dine? Although Jake could have used a good 'ole southern fried dinner made by his step mom, he agreed to dining out! Big mistake! As they walked into Mayor Jacobs' favorite restaurant, Virginia immediately noticed black people were sitting in the back and the whites in the front with large signs appropriately posted, "Whites Only" and

"Blacks Only". Something inside her sparked as she walked proudly to where the blacks were sitting and sat down. The Jacobs' family, except Jake, was shocked and embarrassed. As Virginia waved to them to join her, they sat in the whites section. Jake was torn...what to do? He was beginning to think some of those bombing missions were easier than this. He slowly walked over to talk to Virginia, but she controlled the conversation and he quietly sat down with her amongst the blacks for he knew she was right. He would have hell to pay for this! As they all walked out together, after eating quite a distance from each other, Jake's father whispered in his ear, "Never bring HER back here again!" and he did not! In fact, Jake vowed he would never go back; the segregation was wrong!

When they returned from the south, Jake and Virginia moved into a rental home in San Gabriel, California. From there Virginia continued working for B.F. Goodrich, the tire company. During the war, it manufactured mostly military tires and it continued doing so along with the new demands of personal cars. Jake received his relief from duty on September 27, 1945 and assumed an inactive status with the Eighth Reserve District so he was free to begin work as a Tire Engineer with B.F. Goodrich. He was anxious to begin a regular civilian life and settle into a routine. One thing Jake learned and liked from the military, was a good solid routine. Since a Tire Engineer's job included monitoring wear and tear and sales of tires, he was to travel around the city to the clients. One morning before he left for work, he found

Virginia in the bathroom throwing up her breakfast, getting to her feet and smoothing out her dress to continue getting ready to go to her job. Jake was insistent she should not go to work if she were sick, but she insisted. And when Virginia Lea persists, she will not be stopped. All day Jake worried about her so he arrived home early from work just as she was pulling up in the Chrysler. She threw her arms around him, gave him her sexiest kiss, and said, "I'm pregnant". Although Jake had promised himself to always act strong with no tears, he happily teared-up and swept her off her feet and swung her around! A baby! Life is once again good!

The future parents began spending more time at the Green Valley Lake cabin in the mountains on the weekends. It gave Jake and Virginia time to plan for the baby and their future. During one trip to the cabin, Dorothy came along. It started out to be a peaceful time until Virginia kept pushing her mother's emotional buttons; an eruption of tempers ensued. Jake had never been around two women who could verbally destroy each other. The yelling and insulting stunned Jake. He had been a Marine Corps officer in charge of hundreds of men, none who would ever speak to a senior officer the way Virginia spoke to her mother. Later that evening, he quietly and kindly gave Virginia a piece of his mind about what he had witnessed earlier in the day. She did not take it kindly and began yelling and humiliating him. Jake had always been a quiet, self controlled gentleman and he remained that way throughout the scolding he received to mind his own business and to let her handle her mother how she saw fit. Another lesson learned by Jake; he would have to figure out a way to handle this woman without a huge flare up. However, the emotional impact did not seem to bother Virginia, but it hurt Jake deeply. He only hoped his unborn child was okay.

As the baby grew, so did Jake's dislike for his civilian job, a tire salesman. Never having the personality to sell anything except some tickets for his cousin's barnstorming business in the early 1930's, Jake struggled with the job, his ego, and his wife. Being a woman who liked fine things, Virginia thought sales would make a lucrative career for her often timid husband because a salesman has control over his income by commissions he made. Jake's quiet determination, gentle manner, soft spoken character did not seem to be bringing in the resources Virginia hoped for. Also, Virginia made it quite clear to Jake that she was going to continue to work, even after the baby was born. She loved her work life; the social interactions the job gave her, the stimulation of her mind, the independence of having money. She would not negotiate. She would continue working. Jake would not have a say in the matter. The excitement of the baby kept the couple together and helped Jake to give in to her whims. Surely when the baby was born, she would stay home with it. The very idea of a woman not wanting to care for her own baby was not even thinkable. Everything would be okay, but Jake had to quit his job, but that could not and would not happen until their baby was born. In the meantime, they still lived in San Gabriel and on June 6, 1946, at St. Luke's hospital (now a Cal Tech testing lab) in Pasadena, California, Edward Lee Jacobs was born. Oh, what a blue-eyed, healthy wonder! Jake was a father. He once again did what he promised himself he would never do, he cried.

As Eddie grew, his mommy did not quit work and his daddy could not tolerate another day of selling tires. Fortunately, Jake had an idea of what he could do! San Diego had always been the most beautiful area of California, so Jake thought! That was where he and his wife had become wed, and had their honeymoon. With the blessing of his wife and the help of her mother, Jake began building a house for the new family in the Pacific Beach area of San Diego County. What a perfect location, thanks to Dorothy who bought, sold, and understood properties. She had inherited what the family called, "the Reno Money" a few years before and invested wisely. She was not a timid person. Like her daughter, when she decided to do something, she did it! And thus went Jake in the same direction. He was never one to use tools like hammers, saws, nails and whatever else it takes to actually physically build a house, but he knew how to supervise and he knew how to approve a floor plan. Jake was a planner, thinker, delegator. It worked for him. Virginia even approved of this project using some of her own money as well as Jake's military savings. Between the Green Valley cabin and their future home, Virginia, Jake, and Eddie would be fine. As Virginia said, she did not and would not quit working. She continued working at B.F. Goodrich but at a San Diego location. They were living in a small rental property with excited anticipation of finishing the new house. The plan was to live in the two bedroom lower level and rent out the two bedroom upper level. But, Eddie needed someone to care for him daily and Willie Mae was the answer. As Eddie grew, his main caregiver was the black nanny that fed, cleaned and comforted him daily. Jake had realized Virginia was right; she was not and would never be a nurturing mother. Virginia was okay that Eddie was attached to Willie Mae and not her. Jake spent as much time as he could with Baby Eddie but he was working on a major project: a family home. The day finally came in early 1948 for the move and Jake discovered he did not have an address. No other house had been built on the block so the city asked him what he wanted to name the street. He responded, "Dixie Drive". One block up from the beach at the popular Pacific Beach in sunny southern California, Jake moved his family into the home creating memories that lasted his lifetime; good and bad.

Not three months passed when tragedy struck. Tragedies come in all degrees and in Jake's mind, this was a 9 out of 10! Virginia was driving to Los Angeles to pick Eddie up from his Grandmother Dorothy's house. The Torrey Pines Road curved along steep mountain canyons and ocean cliffs. Not a very wide road at the time, Virginia was driving her new Chrysler Plymouth at 1:30 a.m. A fast driver by habit, she was manipulating the large piece of steel easily through the curves. She had taken this drive many times, mostly to take or pick up her son from her mother's house in Los Angeles.

Eddie and his Grandma seemed to have a special bond; perhaps it was because they had the same family blood, or she spoiled him, or she nurtured him which he was missing from his own mother. Either way, Virginia knew the road. She also knew she was not in a good mood that evening when she left her Dixie Drive home. She and Jake had once again had a disagreement. Actually, she had it. He never really disagreed; he was kind and tried to talk out the problems they had recently been having. She left the house about 9 pm and decided to get into a more melancholy mood by having a martini at her favorite bar in the neighborhood. She thought one would be fine, but then, being the gregarious woman she was, she began talking to people. It felt good to socialize, to let her cares melt away. After a couple more beverages, she realized how late it was and began her drive to pick up her son. As the car careened off the side of the Torrey Pines Road, Virginia felt she was in a whirlpool, going round and round with the sounds of crunching of steel and the snapping of trees. Then, finally, silence!

Jake and Dorothy stood over Virginia at the Balboa Naval Hospital terrified for her life. She had broken bones, scrapes and bruises, but she was alive! This was a #9 tragedy; had she died or Eddie had been with her it would had been a #10. A near miss. As Virginia laid in traction for four months, Jake, Dorothy and Willie Mae took over the duties of raising Eddie, taking care of the house, handling their finances. And Jake had to make a decision about his future job. He had been missing the military. That was really all he knew how to do or wanted to do. He had been successful and respected as a Marine and he had been happy! He knew this would be a hard decision for himself and for his family and he knew Virginia would be dead against it. She was insistent that there was a civilian job for him that would pay him much better and she would not have to be a military wife. After all, they had Eddie now. What kind of a life would that be for him? Jake would wait until his wife came home from the hospital and was fully recovered before he enlisted. He would first find out if the military would take him. Since the war, enlistments were down because the need for men was limited, thank God. No war. He knew one thing for sure; he could not see himself in a civilian job; not now maybe not ever. He was a good Marine. He wanted the routine and respect of military life.

The four months crawled by but the routine on Dixie Drive was functional and for Jake it was a peaceful and content time. He thanked God every day for the heavy steel of the well built Chrysler that saved his wife's life that fateful night. He visited Virginia often and always spoke to her lovingly. He continued to be what he had always been: soft spoken, analytical, diligent, loyal. She continued to be what she had always been: social, outspoken, smart, self centered. So, when Virginia finally came home healed, things did not go well when Jake told Virginia he was enlisting in the Army. The neighbors could hear her screaming and crying for hours. Jake laid out the plan for himself, her and for Eddie. He was a planner and had it all figured out. They would continue to live in the Dixie Drive house during training. When he received his orders, Virginia could decide to come and join him or she could continue staying on Dixie Drive where she could work. Virginia was not happy about it and she certainly did not seem to care about his happiness. Jake knew that if he enlisted it could be the end of his marriage, but was encouraged by Dorothy who, by then, truly adored him. She wanted him to remain married to her daughter. He was by far the best thing to happen to her in her entire life. She understood the selfishness and the needs of her daughter; she had too many arguments with her to be blind to them. Virginia was a tough one to handle; too smart, too beautiful, too much! Jake really did not at the time realize his enlisting again was a death sentence to his marriage, but like always, he thought with true optimism that they would love one another and live together forever, with their handsome, blue-eyed Eddie!

Chapter 12 -- The Enlistment

Jake pondered why he was so unsettled in his new civilian life. Selling tires, building a house and even taking classes at the University of San Diego did not settle him into the life in which he now felt stuck. The marriage had been quite an adjustment for both he and Virginia. They were complete opposites in personalities and habits, but yet, they truly loved one another. After the accident, Jake had a constant feeling of dread; was Virginia loyal? Good for their son? Sober? He did not want to think that any of these were not true, but he just kept getting a nagging feeling inside. He could not control his wife. No one could. With sadness Jake knew how ironic that her independence and determination were two of the reasons he loved her, and also the reasons they may have to part ways. If a woman could be a president of a company or of the United States in the 1940's, Jake was sure Virginia Lea would have become one. She was difficult to live with, but Jake was willing to sacrifice almost anything to remain married to her, except his call to duty.

Since the age of 19 Jake was in the military. He knew nothing else. His way of life was military; he missed the feeling of purpose that the military gave him, the uniform he wore, the camaraderie of his peers, the giving to his country. He became a man in every way as a Marine and his loyalty to the military was just as strong as to his wife, maybe stronger. It is well known that a man who has sworn his life to the U.S.

Military will sacrifice his marriage over his job. Jake was willing to take that step on August 15, 1949 when he enlisted in the U.S. Army with an enlisted rank of Staff Sergeant, a rank higher than the Marines would have given him. With great inner strength and encouragement from Dorothy, he signed the official documents in San Diego with orders to report to Ft. Ord in Northern, California the following week. With a heavy heart he spent time with his son; playing ball, watching cartoons, reading books. He was in awe how quickly Eddie caught on to ideas and his agility was showing signs of being a good athlete some day. All these observances made Dad feel proud and hopeful for his little son's future. Unfortunately, Virginia chose to work longer hours that week and came home late, often with the smell of a martini on her breath. Jake worried for his son with a mother that did not seem to want to take responsibility for her home life, but he knew Dorothy would watch out for Eddie and certainly his surrogate mother, Willie Mae, would too. One thing he did know, Virginia loved her son; she just was not a nurturer. As Jake kissed Eddie, Willie Mae and Dorothy goodbye, he took his bag and walked to the nearest train station leaving the new Chrysler for Virginia and his son. He left with his head held high and with a heavy heart, but a man has to do what a man has to do!

Reporting in at Ft. Ord, Jake began to feel a sense of comfort he had not felt since he was relieved of active duty almost three years before. He could smell the discipline, the routine, the purpose of a mission. He was home! After several weeks, the processing and waiting for his first assignment was over with orders to report to Fort Lewis, Washington located near Tacoma. He would be part of the regimental combat team, 4th RCT. The familiar clickity-clack of a train lulled him to sleep as he relaxed on his way to his first Army assignment. How many trains had he ridden on during his first nine years of military service? So many, that Jake felt he had made the right decision for himself and for his family. Upon arrival at Ft. Lewis, he reported into Company E, 2nd Battalion which was commanded by Captain Frank Olander. Receiving his billeting instructions, he was to settle in and report back the following morning giving Jake time to call home to Dixie Drive. His bright and literate Eddie answered the phone which almost melted Jake's heart. Hearing him helped him to realize how important it was that he was once again fighting for the country that his little boy lived in. The security of the country and the personal freedoms were the most important thing for his son. He savored that thought and knew it to be true giving him even more of a clear vision of his mission.

The First Sergeant and Jake became fast friends for he too was a southerner in the midst of mostly northerners in the battalion. The friendly Mississippian had a thick southern drawl and he had a hard time believing Jake was from Arkansas because he certainly talked like a west coast guy. Jake finally proved the southern boy part of him by sharing cultures of the south like grits and eventually, Jake found his birth certificate and proved it once and for all.

They were friends for life. The training took a whole new turn for Jake who had Marine training of land, water and air. Being a pilot, his training was very different from the training that he was about to have—winter training located on Mt. Rainier. Jake had thought he saw the most beautiful landscape in the world on the California beach, but he was just as captivated and awed by the sight of Mt. Rainier. What a spectacular mountain set in the lush evergreen forests of the state of Washington. He and his battalion set up training camp at the mid elevation, about 8,000 feet, and were issued winter gear including a pair of skis. Skis? Really? Jake had never been close to a pair of skis much less put them on. As they bunked in that evening, all the skis issued to the men were lined up against the tent, haunting each member of the battalion during their sleep. Skis, oh my! Good news, there was no snow; not yet! However, the snow began to fall and so did the battalion as they each learned to ski beginning on the beginner's hill. Ski training and exercises continued until each man could make it down the steep slopes without falling too much. He did not mind a fast plane, but fast skis? Wow! Not the rush like that SB2C. Jake never felt real secure on skis, but the snowshoes training went better. They were easier to learn and slower although more awkward and cumbersome too, but they had their purpose. After six weeks of this winter training, the battalion returned to Ft. Lewis with sore muscles in places they never thought they had muscles. The purpose of all the winter training came when Jake received his assignment to go to Alaska. Ahhh! Skis and snowshoes. Sounded like a chilling experience. But, before he left he had a few days off, so he hurried back to see his wife and son.

Nothing much had changed in the house at Dixie Drive except Eddie was bigger and more talkative, in fact, he talked a lot. Jake was okay with that as he was only three years old and could not say his r's or l's very well. He told Jake, "Daddy, I wuv you." And once again, Jake's heart melted. He knew his new Army career would mean missing some important developmental times in his son's life. That was the hard part. The hardest part was that he thought he would also miss Virginia. If only they could spend some special times together like they use to. Virginia, once again, was not around when he visited home. He only got a quick couple hours with her because between her social engagements (whatever they were) and her job. She had no time for him, or for her son.

Jake returned a few hours early to Ft. Lewis so he decided to take a trip up to Seattle to do some necessary shopping and perhaps to buy a beer to be by himself to ponder his life as a soldier, father, and husband. He was struggling and being pulled by the tensions of home and his renewed energy in the Army. He loved his job and his family, but he was stressed. Not one to talk it out, he kept it to himself and said a prayer for the safety of his son. Walking to Nordstrom's to take a look at the gloves he needed for the cool mornings in this Northwest climate, he was approached by the saleswoman. She was not ugly, but not pretty. She wore practical clothing, nothing sexy about her. She had a nice smile and seemed friendly but business like. As she showed Nelson the various gloves that might fit his needs he noticed her nails were clean, not painted, her voice was intelligent, not articulate, her hair was brown, not auburn. She was assertive, Jake assumed, for a woman to be a salesperson she would need to have confidence and nerve. Her name was Alice and she had moved from Missouri with her brother and worked at Nordstrom's department store for the past year or so. Jake wondered why she didn't wear the stylish gloves that women in the 1940's so often wore; Virginia would have. While Jake was trying to decide on the pair of gloves he liked the best, Alice was busily talking with another gentleman. Jake was brought into the conversation with Alice because the man was a soldier that had just finished winter training at Mt. Rainier. Trading light hearted stories of the training and WWII, they all three became fast friends. They agreed to meet again, only socially, when they could coordinate time. They exchanged numbers and went their separate ways. At least for the time being.

The orders to go to Alaska were delayed due to the unrest in Korea, mostly caused by the Americans and our Allies to stop Communism before it could take over the world. Because of the starting of the Korean War in 1950, they were given the assignment of helping to deploy the 2nd Division which had been alerted for deployment to Korea. It took a month to get all the division on its way. The Army then found out that there were no troops left on the West coast for defense purposes and Jake's battalion had to once again delay Alaska in order to wait until a National Guard division could be activated and moved to Fort Lewis from Minnesota. When they arrived, finally the deployment to Alaska occurred. With all the delays, Jake had the opportunity to reunite with his Seattle Nordstrom's friends several times. They went different places such as the chilly coast of Washington for salmon dinners, a hike into the forests of the Pacific Northwest, dinners and lunches on the Seattle waterfront, ferry rides across the Hood Canal, and even target practice. Eventually, it was just Alice and Jake going on adventures together. Jake was not being disloyal to his wife, Alice and he were friends. Nothing for Virginia to worry about for, certainly, there was nothing sexy about Alice. However, Jake did find some qualities in Alice that were lacking in his wife and which he highly respected; she liked order, cooking, the outdoors, interest in Jake's activities. Although he found that Alice seemed to have a mean streak, he actually had fun being with Alice and didn't mind how she was a fanatic about things being in order and on time. He was military, he liked those things too. She even fussed over him one evening during dinner because he was pale with a slight fever. Being a man that never complained, she figured it out by herself. Virginia would never have noticed or cared. Nevertheless, it was nice to have such a good friend who cared.

Jake continued his letters and phone calls home. Sometimes he was a little chagrin when no one was home and it was night time. Those times he would call Dorothy and be relieved that Eddie was with her. "Thank God for Grandmothers," Jake would think but where was his wife? There were times he wondered if he had made the right decision to join the Army. He had begged his wife to bring his son to be with him during his trainings. They could have lived in military housing and they could have been together, but she refused. She had a life and the military was not part of it he was told. It hurt. He had been hurt before; years before. How did he keep falling in love with these women who were not loyal? He sure knew how to pick 'em. He decided before he was shipped to Alaska he would approach Virginia and face their marriage solution.

He had to go to 9th Avenue in Los Angeles to see his son and wife. That is where they spent most their time, or at least it was where Eddie spent most of his time, with his Grandmother. Oh, how Eddie loved his Grandmother. Jake was delighted to see the shining smile on his son's face, his little arms reaching high to be picked up, the way he could run…just like Jake when he was a young lad. Oh, the joy he felt when he saw his son. Where was Virginia? For five days, Jake was made welcome by Dorothy and Herbie, her husband. Dorothy cooked for him and counseled him about her daughter. She encouraged him to show his tenacity and strength, to go out and reel her in by force if necessary. Jake sat for hours at a time and waited. He would not and could not force her to love him or to stay with him. He contemplated, prayed, played with Eddie. Virginia never showed. It was over. Not just by his choice, because that is not what he wanted; it was to be. A divorce was inevitable and he was heartbroken. Virginia was just too much of everything, except loving. Thank God for Dorothy for Jake knew as long as she was around Eddie would always be okay. He also knew there would be a day of reckoning, for he refused to give up his son. Someday, when he was able, he would get custody of his child and, oh, what a day that would be!

Chapter 13 – From Trophies to Alaska and Back Again!

Alice was not the trophy that Virginia was, but what exactly is a trophy anyway? A trophy does not love you, care for you, cook your meals, listen to your problems, and nurture you. But a trophy can be enjoyable to win and possess. Displayed in public a trophy can look good on your arm, be fun and engaging. His trophy wife was gone and now Jake needed a mate. Even though he knew Alice could not have children, out of convenience, loneliness and rebound, Jake asked Alice to marry him. She accepted and vowed she would wait for him to come back to Seattle from Alaska. She even promised as soon as they were married she would go with him to whatever assigned base he was stationed. She would stand by his side and be his wife and look after his welfare. Jake had the feeling he finally found a good one, or at least, a loyal one!

Jake kissed Alice goodbye as he boarded a transport ship to Alaska. The vessel sailed through the Inland Passage along the Canadian Coast to the port of Whittier on the Alaskan coast which had been built during World War II by the Army engineers. From Whittier the battalion traveled to Fairbanks on the Alaska Railroad. It was rugged country but beautiful. Once again Jake was struck by the grandeur and beauty of America. Right when he thought there could be no more beautiful of a place than the California coast, there was

Mt. Rainier, and then there was Alaska. He was awe struck! Another 25 mile trip by bus from Fairbanks landed him at their destination, the Eielson Air Force base. It was October of 1950 and the snow was on the ground and the air was icy. The mission was to protect the airbase. Since the Cold War was fully engaged with Russia, the United States feared the USSR may attack us on our own land. The closest way to do that would be to cross the Bering Strait which became an ice bridge connecting the USSR and the United States during the winter. The U.S. viewed this as a real threat. In the middle of November, Jake found himself with 20 other officers at Big Delta, Alaska at the Arctic Training Center for the Instructors course in Arctic Survival and warfare. Jake thought skiing was a challenge; he was in for far more intense training. The instructors were U.S. Army recruits from Finland. These men helped to defeat the Russians when they first invaded Finland in 1939 but Finland was overcome by sheer numbers of Russians. Until then, the Finns gave the Russians a sound shellacking. They had learned a lot about how to survive the cold and warfare and they were brutal. They were hard task masters but that month was well spent. Jake learned about fighting and surviving under extreme cold weather conditions It was then Jake's and the other officers responsibility to instruct their respective units in the conduct of arctic war fare. Fighting in 50 degree below zero weather is rough and without knowledge, proper training and 110% effort you could easily die.

One early morning Chaplain Tom of the base asked Jake

over breakfast if he would like to do a little snowshoeing with him. Jake liked the Chaplain and figured it could never hurt to hang out with the God fearing fellow, so he said that sounded nice. He was just happy he didn't ask him to go skiing with him; Jake decided he hated skiing. They dressed warmly and began chugging across the ice covered tundra. Jake trustingly followed the Chaplain. They stopped periodically to eat some snow, snack on some rations and as they slowly snow-shoed along they talked about many things. Jake thoroughly was enjoying his time with this God-like man. They had gone a few miles and as they sat down to snack, the Chaplain said, "Welcome to Russia." What? No! Jake did not believe his ears. What was he talking about? The Chaplain quietly explained they had crossed half over the ice bridge of the Bering Strait and had crossed the border into Russia. Jake jumped up and wished he had been skiing because he could not make those snowshoes move fast enough to get back across the border of the United States. Jake figured it was a near miss! The Chaplain followed laughing all the way. Jake figured even a Chaplain has to do naughty things now and then and the joke was on Jake. There were no guards, planes, or even a living creature of any kind that saw them on that crystal blue sky day that was 60 degrees below zero.

After completing one of the most difficult months of his life on December 16, 1950, he returned to Eielson Air Force Base. Looking back on the month he had just spent, he reflected on how different his military career had been. From bombing missions in the sweltering hot Pacific to protecting the snow covered below freezing Alaskan land as a foot soldier, to crossing the Russian border. Amazing.

Jake was soon transferred to battalion headquarters as the battalion operations Sergeant. He had been promoted while away at Big Delta to Master Sergeant. It was not a gift. He had worked hard for it. In his new assignment he was working with a Major and a Lt. Colonel. They worked together well and the rank was rarely apparent. Getting the job done was all that mattered. They were responsible for the training and planning of the operations assigned to the battalion. One of the operations they planned and executed was taking the entire battalion on a field exercise during which the temperature never reached above 50 degrees below zero. Cold, cold, cold!

Then, with a promotion to First Lieutenant, Jake once again held the rank with which he left the Marine's. His diligence, demeanor, loyalty earned him the rank giving service in the coldest areas of the United States protecting the border. He had once again proven himself as a capable and strong leader. After a short time at Fort Richardson near Anchorage, Jake was transferred to the Ladd Army Airfield in the Fairbanks area to be the executive Officer of Company A, 1st Battalion with duties including supply officer. Fortunately, he was given a few days leave to go back to Seattle and finish what he promised.

On February 13th, 1951 in the State of Washington, Alice Snyder became Jake's bride. Alice quit her job at Nordstrom's after buying some very warm clothing, including gloves, for her honeymoon and new life on a military base in Alaska. She relished the idea of having a husband and looked forward to the times ahead including seeing new sights. She was ecstatic to finally go to Alaska. Jake knew this wife would take care of the home front and be with him for always for who would agree to live in Alaska during the winter if she was anything but in love and loyal?

The adventures of being married to Alice began with the very small one bedroom hut which was difficult to move about. With only a few weeks of this close living, too close even for honeymooners, Alice met someone that knew of a vacant and roomier log house with electricity and heat from the city's heating plant. They grabbed it. Jake was amazed by Alice's assertiveness to get the deal done, but unlike his previous wife, it was done for the good of the couple! As they were getting comfortable in their new home, Alice found a job on base at the PX keeping her busy and still available for Jake. One evening as they were having a quiet dinner in their home, something they both cherished, sirens blazed. It broke the serene silence of the Alaskan environment. A two story Fairbanks building was in flames. Alice and Jake ran out into the street to see it up close, along with many other curious neighbors; after all, that is what people do! Alice noticed a young couple standing in their night clothes, staring and looking frightened. She approached them to find they were tourists from Florida and everything was in the burning building, including their money, credit cards, clothes. The Jacobs' couple led them to their log cabin, tucked them into the second bedroom and addressed their needs the following day. After finding them clothing and contacts at the local bank to get money, the couple stayed in the log cabin for the remainder of their stay. The couple was an inspiration for Alice and Jake to go out and enjoy some of the local activities such as the dog sled races. Jake learned a lot about his wife during that time. She not only looked out for him, but also, her fellow American. She was not a fuzzy warm woman by any means, she was rough around the edges, and sometimes quite cruel with remarks showing a mean streak now and then, but she did rise to the occasion when someone needed help. Jake respected that.

The days grew warmer and the days grew longer with only a couple hours of dark during the summer months. The annual midnight baseball game was played with lighting from the midnight sun, the salmon spawned by swimming upstream so thick one could not see the water and the herds of buffalo were so large the game warden had to move herds out of the area on a regular basis. All these Jake was fascinated by and his wife was by his side enjoying them as well.

One September day, Jake received a phone call notifying him of two Gold Medals that he earned during his service as a Marine in the Pacific. In Los Angeles, the two Gold Medals arrived at 9th Avenue because that was the last address the Marine Corps had for Jake. Dorothy was so excited for Jake and for Eddie that she raced to the local elementary school, burst into the Kindergarten classroom, found her grandson, pulled him to the front of the class, asked the teacher permission to show the class something important and proceeded to show Eddie his father's medals. She glowed with pride. She explained to the class as well as her grandson a Gold Medal is for honor and valor for military duty during combat. Eddie, although he was embarrassed in front of the whole class, was happy! He received a lot of ice cream that night, just because his Daddy was a hero! Worked for him.

Dorothy called Fairbanks as soon as she returned from the school. As Jake answered the phone and heard Dorothy's voice, fear struck him. What was wrong? Is Edward okay? But, her voice was so excited. She was squealing, "You received two Gold Medals". Jake quietly listened and felt a sense of pride. He had not expected that. Although he was proud of the medals, Jake never liked to blow his own horn. Bragging and talking about himself was in his eyes, narcissistic. Dorothy told him how she went to find Eddie to show him and that he, too, was very proud of his Daddy. Jake felt proud inside but never a man to brag, only quietly told Alice about the phone call adding, "The government must have a big backup of paperwork since the war ended six years ago." Alice was so excited and proud of Jake for his medals, she treated him to dinner at his favorite steak house in Fairbanks with a couple glasses of champagne and a continuation of celebration at home in their bedroom.

Orders arrived for Jake in October of 1952 to report to Fort Benning, Georgia for the Company Officers Course. Saying goodbye to the beautiful Alaskan territory was a little sad for Alice and Jake. Alaska seemed to allow them to find their niche with each other. But, being military one goes where one is ordered to go, and Alice had no problem with that. The excitement of the next experience seemed to motivate her. Although she had only a 6th grade education and been raised on a farm in Missouri, she was always up for an adventure. Their first months together as a couple had gone well. Alice accepted Jake's need for a calm existence in the house, accepted his love for his son, made friends with other officers' wives and graciously hosted dinners at their home. Alice was proving to be a good wife, and loyal too! Once again Jake felt his life was falling into place; he only wished he could be more accessible to his son. He made expensive long distance calls to check on him and sent birthday and Christmas gifts. He was anxious to get back to the continental United States in hopes to spend some time with him. It would not be possible for a while.

Chapter 14: Continental United States and Edward

Fort Benning was the most populated base to which Jake had ever been. The Infantry and Army schools were located there so it was a beehive of activity. The schools were attended by all the U. S. services and many military men from foreign countries; mostly South and Central America. To Jake, it was organized chaos. As Jake began his classes he realized there was a schedule that needed to be met, information that had to be learned. Once again as in all military institutions, every i was dotted and every t was crossed. Exact. Punctual. Once Jake settled in, he enjoyed the learning and the order to what he had first believed to be chaos. Six months of courses in all phases of military subjects, Jake graduated and was assigned to Camp Roberts located about 100 miles south of San Francisco. Yipee! He would at last be able to connect with his son and once again be on the California coast. At his side, he had Alice.

Camp Roberts was a training center and so the activities were always fluid; continual changes. When Jake reported in he was assigned to the G4 Section of the 7th Armored Division, commanded by General Robert F. Sink, nicknamed Bourbon Bob. Jake had to wonder about that nickname but he figured it was sort of obvious. Bourbon Bob was a rugged type that expected the most from everyone. Not surprisingly, he had advanced his way up to General. Jake and the General got to know each other fairly well and Jake firmly believed 'ole Bourbon Bob needed a junior officer for his odd jobs that none of the incumbents wanted to do. Jake always took orders, followed the rules, was a true military type guy, and because of those qualities on June 30, 1953 he was promoted to Captain. Soon after, notification came that Camp Roberts was to be closed and the facility turned over to the National Guard for their use and the Army would use other bases for training. Also, the Korean War was winding down and fewer training bases would be required. Jake was called in to see the General and was given the responsibility for closing down the post promptly and no one would be permitted to cause a delay. This would not be an easy task for Jake, but he was up for it. Jake loved organization. He loved a challenge. He set up camp in the Uthili Atoll, he could certainly break one down! Each morning at 7 am there would be a briefing in the General's office including all the commanders and Jake would provide a status report. Problem areas would be discussed and commanders would have to explain their delays. Jake was the one responsible for being on the General's list, so, within a few days everyone knew who Jake was. Needless to say, he was not always the most popular kid on the block, but he got the job done. At the end, Jake received two sets of orders. One was back to advanced training classes at Fort Benning and the other to the Presidio at San Francisco for duty until time to report to Fort Benning. For five months, Jake and Alice enjoyed the sights, sounds, tastes of San Francisco. With not much expected of him on the base, Jake enrolled in afternoon classes at San Francisco State University and managed to get in 15 semester hours to satisfy his learning craze. Alice encouraged him and began a new hobby; oil painting. After having spent time in Alaska and now in the intriguing beautiful San Francisco area, she wanted to capture on canvas her experiences. She was talented and she was content.

Jake's great desire to see his son became a reality in the summer of 1954. Eddie was already eight years old with too much emotional baggage for anyone of that young age. Virginia was remarried to an engineer and had moved her son to Tulerosa, New Mexico where her husband worked as a contractor for the Air Force. Of course, Jake could not even begin to imagine his ex wife living in a remote town away from the Pacific Ocean, so he was not surprised when after two more children, Virginia and her husband moved to San Diego where her new husband worked for Ryan Aviation. The shock of Virginia having two more kids also shook up Jake. Some people should not have children and Jake firmly believed Virginia was one of them; although he was happy to have Eddie. Although Jake had made phone calls to Eddie's grandmother, he could not be part of his son's life while in Alaska or Ft. Benning. In the 1950's air travel was not common and atrociously expensive, long distance phone calls were spendy, to say the least, but Jake finally had his chance. Although grateful for Dorothy, she was not an easy hombre to deal with. Since he had arrived in Fort Roberts he had been begging to see his son. It was difficult because he lived in New Mexico with his mother, and his mother was not co operative about such things like what was best for her children. Finally, Jake got wind that Eddie would be moving to San Diego with his family and that is when he negotiated the week to receive time with his son. Come to find out later, Virginia was more than happy to have "Eddie" stay with Grandma for a few weeks, because, after all, she was tired. She was back in her "hood" so to speak with places to go and things to do and work to find; and she had two little ones to care for. Although her Eddie was a big help playing and watching the little ones, he was an active eight year old and, thankfully Grandma wanted him. Jake drove down to 9th Avenue and finagled his son from the grasp of his doting Grandmother and drove him back to Fort Roberts before Dorothy could think of a reason he couldn't go. Not that Jake blamed Dorothy; she was Edward's protector and nurturer. Thank God.

Alice was not an animal lover or child lover. Jake knew that from the beginning, but she was willing to have Jake's son who he missed so much spend a week with them. She was strict, rather cold, but that was mostly because she was never around children. She was actually thankful she could not have children. So, this was her step son and she would feed him and be as kind as she could be. They discussed that they should call Eddie, Edward, his formal name. The week went well and Jake spent every minute he could with his son. He even took him into work with him a couple days and Edward followed his father around the base like a puppy taking in everything his father did. His only other male figure had been Doug, his stepfather, and his step grandfather, Herbie. This was exciting for Edward to be so close to his father. Jake's demeanor was the same around everyone, including his son. Soft spoken, firm but kind with discipline, analytical. Edward didn't mind. He was eight and he liked the activity of the base. One day he was playing outside his dad's office with another boy; first playing some catch and then they found a rattlesnake. As young boys do, they did not recognize the real danger in a rattler but they did recognize the fun. As they chased the snake around, trying to catch it, Jake glanced out his office window not expecting to see what he saw. Totally mortified, he jumped to his feet, ran out and grabbed both boys by the arms, drug them away from the irritated rattlesnake, calmly and quietly with a steady voice told them not to move, and handled the snake himself. The snake did not make it. Alice did not cook it. In fact, that evening they all went out for vanilla ice cream. A lot of ice cream. Father and son's favorite food. Every time Jake saw a snake after that day, he thought of his blue-eyed blond headed little boy so close to danger! Being the only near fatal incident of the week, with sadness, yet gratefulness in his heart, Jake returned his son to grandma's house promising to make more calls to him. Edward was pleased.

The advanced course at Fort Benning was quite a bit tougher than Jake's first one. The students were older, had more time in the service, more experienced and for the most part more formally educated. There was a lot of homework and a great deal of time was spent in simulated field conditions. It was a course for officers who possessed the skills required to be agile and adaptive leaders and had the knowledge to confidently conduct operations across various environments. That was a course for Jake and inside, he felt he was a soldier who deserved this respect. He was also ecstatic to learn. With the opportunities for army training and university courses, Jake began to soak in as much knowledge about academics and real life as he could. Finishing the top third of his class, he earned a 30 day leave.

Chapter 15: So long Alice, Hello Korea!

Thirty days in Seattle, Washington was spent well. Alice and Jake bought a house in Tacoma, connected with old friends from Ft. Lewis, enjoyed the fresh Northwest air, and moved in just in time for Jake to say "so long" to his wife. He had orders to go to Korea, his next duty station. Because Korea was an unstable country, military families could not accompany their spouses, so Alice stayed behind for the first time in their married life. Jake looked forward to his new mission, but knew he would miss Alice. He had learned to love this caring but sometimes very controlling woman. She made him content although not necessarily happy. He left with Alice working at the PX at Ft. Lewis and a paint brush in her hand. She would have to be patient and wait. That, she was good at. Jake would have to wait to see her again and he would have a long wait to see his son.

The flight from Travis Air Force Base in California to Japan in a military transport plane was a miserably long one with stops in Honolulu and the airbase on Guam. Jake was never overly fond of the transport planes, especially over water. Also, the memories of Japan were still fresh in his memory, so the flight seemed more of a torture than a trip to a new army experience, especially when he was served rations instead of a real meal on the way. A few days in Japan at an American Air Force Base were spent waiting for transportation, orientation and issuance of equipment including a weapon. He was told he would be a courier and would be escorted to the airport to receive whatever needed including an armed escort to Korea. To his amazement, when he reached the airport he was escorted to an airplane and then a truck pulled up and began to load about 200 sealed canvas bags containing classified material. Under no condition was Jake to let them out of his control. Well! Interesting. Jake was the only passenger since it was a courier flight. In two hours his plane landed in Seoul, Korea and he was able to surrender the cargo to another officer authorized to receive it. He was glad to have completed his first assignment in Korea as he climbed aboard a jeep driven by a warrant officer and the administrative officer for the G4 Section, Headquarters, U. s. 8th Army. In the Army as it does in civilian life, your experience follows you. After settling into his quarters, Jake realized how much larger of an operation it was than the one at Camp Roberts. The next morning work began before 7 am and Jake's desk already had an overflowing in-box. He was taken on a tour of the headquarters then dropped back to his office and left on his own. It was a matter of sink or swim. He elected to swim.

Jake's division was responsible for supplying the entire Army. Of course, they did not do that by themselves, there were seven different technical services operating as independent units that did the actual work. The directions and guidance came from Jake's unit, G4, but the responsibility for the entire 8th Army belonged to General Ondrick, his boss.

Actually Jake had expected an assignment to the

DMZ (Demilitarized Zone) when he arrived in Korea, so he was pleasantly surprised he was sent to Headquarters. He assumed his staff experience had something to do with it. At any rate, he was overjoyed since the living conditions were better including the food, which was always a major factor in his life! Working for Colonel Duke Ondrick, Jake was once again junior office in the section. It all worked out well as the junior received many special projects that otherwise he would not have gotten. They included many flights to outlying areas for inspections and investigations, several trips to Japan for meetings on subjects about which he knew very little except what he could learn from papers received just prior to departing. Some Army, huh? However, it was a great learning experience and Jake figured it could come in useful someday. On his return he took over the job of a Major who had returned to the states. Lucky him. Jake had inherited a job that caused a lot of people to be mad at him. They could not always get what they wanted; not even generals.

Unannounced meetings became a specialty. It seemed that whenever Jake's division leader did not want to attend a meeting, he would give a wave and off Jake would go! This included several trips to Japan so it wasn't all minuses; in fact there were some pluses. One of the pluses was spending a week in Japan and loafing around like a tourist exploring the small towns, temples, riding the crowded trains and even had a hot bath in a family bathhouse. Strictly family! Jake was taken back in time as he gazed at the famed Bronze

Budha. Returning to Japan was like returning to a different world since Japan was being rebuilt and the people were no longer under a tyrant.

An incident occurred one day while trying to catch up after being away for a couple of days. He looked up from his desk and there stood an old friend from Fort Lewis and Alaska. He was the G4 of his division and was in Seoul to see Jake. He handed Jake a special requisition and explained to Jake that his commander, General Carraway, wanted the requisition hand carried and wanted an immediate response. Both Jake's friend and he knew what the answer would be, but, Jake called the Quartermaster and asked for an immediate check on the equipment; helmet liners. There were Helmet liners in the warehouses in Korea. After checking on the amount availability, Jake informed his Colonel friend that the answer would be "no". The Colonel left with the emphatic reply, "General Carraway is not going to like this." The helmet liners which the division commander wanted totaled 25,000 and his troops already had one each. He wanted another set so each of them could be painted with the division insignia and worn on parades and in Honor Guards. To Jake that was just another burden for the troops plus a high monetary cost to pay to satisfy some one's ego. His General agreed with him and told Jake that if the guy showed up again to send him in to his office. Sure enough, the guy appeared again and into General Ondrick's office he went. End of problem. Jake found it interesting that General Carraway was the son of Senator Hattie Carraway of Arkansas. He always thought people from Arkansas were smarter than that; Fortunately, Jake new General Carraway's father was much smarter.

One of the meetings he was sent to, he sat in on the negotiation of the Third Military Railroad Service (TMRS) which was the railroad in Korea. The war was over but the U. S. Military retained control of the railroad which was built by the Army Engineers. On July 27, 1953 an armistice was agreed upon ending the active conflict in Korea. To show good will, the TMRS assisted and trained the Koreans in rebuilding and maintaining the railway system. Jake became a major player in this negotiation that led to the eventual railway control by the Koreans and the newly named Korean National Railway. During the meeting, the General facilitating the meeting revealed the proficient intelligence of the Army by turning to Jake and saying, "Your grandfather was a railroad guy, you know more about railroads than any of us. You are in charge." Baffled, Jake always obeyed orders and asked for a recess of the meeting so he could go learn about what he supposedly already knew about the railway. Studying briefing notes, historical news reports and settling his nerves, the meeting resumed the next day. Throughout negotiations Jake kept his calm, soft spoken, intelligent demeanor and finalized the deal. What a feat, especially since all he knew about his grandfather (Nelson Edward Jacobs 1846 – 1933) was that his trade was a telegrapher, he had an adventuring spirit, enlisted in the Confederate Army during the Civil War and was in Leavenworth Prison after being captured just a couple weeks after enlisting. He remained there until the end of the war. He then became a Pony Express rider and a railroad man; mostly sending telegraphs and helping now and then laying some track. Interesting fellow, but Jake could not for the life of him figure how that made him qualified to help with a railroad negotiation or how the Army knew about his grandfather. The Army! Want to gain new experiences without a moment's notice? Join the Army.

Since Alice was not able to join Jake during his 17 months in Korea, he spent most of his evenings going to school since University of California-Berkley had a campus in Seoul. Not only did Jake quench his thirst for knowledge, but he racked up 24 semester hours. Eighteen hour days were the norm for Jake during that time, but what else was there to do? Work, learn, and eat! But, the day finally came for him to return home to his Washington house in which he had never lived for a 30 day leave, then off to Fort Jackson, South Carolina!

Chapter 16: Home Again, Home Again, Jiggity-Jig!

After a two hour flight from Seoul to Japan, Jake was booked on an Air Force flight from Tokyo to Travis Air Force Base near San Francisco. After two aborted takeoffs and a change of planes, he was on his way home. As were all Air Force Trans Pacific flights, it was long. It was difficult for Jake to get comfortable, not just because of the unnerving beginning of the flight and the uncomfortable seats, but once again he was flying over the Islands he had bombed. He was good at repressing memories, so as they kept popping up in his head as he looked out the window he dismissed them. Even the memories came back of his first love back in Arkansas. He shook his head, and had to remind himself to learn from the past, do not dwell on it. Live for today. Look to the future. And his future was once again promising. He had learned many life skills that would help him in his job. His mind was alert from studying at the university and his heart was content with his wife at home. As the plane flew over that huge Pacific with stops at Wake Island and Honolulu, he was also worrying about his son, Edward. Word was out that Edward's mother sent him to military school for 3rd grade. Jake could not for the life of him wrap his head around the idea of sending a youngster to a school like that! Since Virginia had sole custody of their son, neither Jake nor Dorothy could do a damn thing about it! It sickened Jake to think his son was basically imprisoned at Mount Lowe Military School in Altadena, California. As Jake reflected about his boot camp at age 19, he wondered how does an eight year old cope with that? What prompted this? The only answer he could get from Virginia was that Eddie was incorrigible. What? Edward had spent a week with Jake and Alice just a month before he was put at the school. He was not incorrigible; he was an active, smart, normal eight year old boy. Dorothy agreed but neither could stop Virginia once she got an idea in her stubborn head. What was more disturbing to Jake was the fact that Edward's mother never even visited him during his third grade year; the only visitor being Dorothy. To unnerve Jake more was the fact that his son was living with his Grandmother and Herbie in Los Angeles attending 4th grade at the local school. Jake knew it was a better place for him, but how could a mother be so unfeeling towards her son? What does all that instability do to Edward? He must really have felt abandoned! Jake remembered how upset he was to find out his aunt was not his real mother at age 19, but at least he had a mother around him; stability, security. What could Jake do? This made it even more important to Jake to be going back to the states.

Jake had just enough time in Seattle to reconnect with his wife in their new home; not so new to Alice anymore as she had been living in it for the past year and a half. She had made it a home, not just a house. Many of her oil paintings adorned the house, all their belongings were arranged in an orderly but comfortable fashion and Alice was happy to make home cooked meals for Jake; Jake was happy to eat them. The time went fast and Jake did not get his visit with

Edward because Virginia refused to let him "disrupt" his life. Jake was furious; even tried to get Dorothy to let him go and see him. She was willing, but the timing was off! Herbie had been spending a lot of time with Edward and she felt a disruption of a visit at that time might be emotionally hard for him. However, Jake did talk to Edward as much as he could between his school and playing baseball with his friends and going to Dodger games with his step grandfather. Jake accepted this and was content for the time being. He was thankful a good man like Herbie was in his son's life. Time ran out and off to Fort Jackson, South Carolina by car, Chrysler of course. Alice would be with him during this assignment.

Chapter 17:   Fort Jackson

As Jake took on his assignment as Company commander, Co. B, 14th BN 3rd Training Regiment, Alice took on the task of making family housing a warm environment and securing a PX job to keep her busy. One thing about Alice, she was not afraid of hard work. Something Jake loved in the gal. She did not let Jake get out of any of the work at home either; she expected him to do his part, but overall, she had proven to be a good wife as far as supporting Jake's endeavors and looking out for his well being. She didn't exactly pamper him. That was not her style!

The mission of Jake's company was to train newly inducted personnel and turn them into soldiers in a very short eight week time period. Many of the enlisted men were coming into the Army from the poverty areas of big cities and the small towns out in the country. Some had not graduated from high school, some had. Most enlisted because they could not get a job and the Army paid. Also, some had their eyes on college but could not afford it. Spending a few years in the Army would give them a resume and money for college through the GI Bill. Some of the young men had not learned the basics of caring for themselves and needed very fundamental training such as brushing their teeth and other personal hygiene skills. Jake was always flabbergasted by the lack of training in those areas and it just added to the stress of there never seeming to be enough time to turn these young kids into soldiers which resulted in long hours for everyone; both trainees and trainers. Overall, Jake and the other trainers felt they did a good job. But there was never a dull moment.

Jake was constantly reminded that the Army keeps a man on his toes, always. Never know what would happen next. One morning after having been on the rifle range beginning at 6 am, Jake decided to go back to the company area for lunch and catch up on some paperwork. Jake believed his mess hall was the best on the post! Food was always important to him, a lot of it, and really, it was important to most of the men. Not only could they fill their stomachs but they could rest their bones for a little while. As Jake drove into the area of the mess hall, he saw a group of people standing outside of one of the barracks. They were pointing and yelling at someone on the roof. Jake soon identified the person as one of his trainees. He would not come down regardless of all of the pleading. The Chaplain was talking to him, but still, he refused to budge. Someone had already sent for the medics just in case he decided to jump since the roof top was a few stories high. Since he belonged to Jake, he joined in the pleas for him to come down. This went on for at least an hour, but to no avail. Meanwhile, the crowd got larger and noisier and Jake ran out of things to say. Finally, impulsively he blurted out, "Private, we're all going to the mess hall and eat. We have fried chicken and I'm not going to miss it, how about you?" So Jake waved everyone toward the mess hall and they all started off in that direction. All of a sudden it dawned on

Jake, "What if the lad does jump and Jake would be booted out of the army for using poor judgment in letting a man kill himself." But, after walking only a short distance, Jake looked around only to see in the chow line was the Private that had been on the roof. Jake really did not enjoy the fried chicken that day after the emotional turmoil that young man caused. After lunch Jake had the Chaplain take the Private to the hospital for an examination. As for himself, Jake told his First Sergeant not to look for him the rest of the day; he was going home and would not be back until the next morning. He had had enough! That was an unforgettable day, but not the last time he saw the Private. A couple weeks later who should knock on his office door? Yup! The man from the roof was reporting back to finish his training. He did finish, but Jake made him go completely through the next training cycle tacking on an extra eight weeks. Jake had to hand it to the young man; after an emotional meltdown, he opted to become a soldier. Good for him! That took guts and perseverance. Jake respected that!

Jake received a call one day from the processing center and was informed that the following week he would receive a new shipment of trainees. "No problem." Jake had replied, but then was told the trainees were from Puerto Rico and, surprise, spoke only Spanish. Jake's cadre (a group of professionals as himself) hit the ceiling when Jake gave them the news. The trainers thought they did not have enough time with the English speakers, but good grief, it was worse with non English speakers. However, the trainers found that once the non English speakers learned the commands, everything else was pretty much physical. The Spanish speaking trainees also learned quickly if they did not follow the commands, they were punished with extra pushups or some horrible manual task like cleaning toilets. They learned and the job was completed. All the trainers took the next week off. They needed the rest.

It's hard to believe that Jake would be considered to have a big mouth or be impulsive, but although he usually chose his words carefully, he too made mistakes. Jake and other officers had an after duty meeting of the pistol and rifle club one night and General Costello showed up unannounced. They had completed their meeting and Jake asked the General if he would like to say something to the group. Of course he did, so he stood up to the podium. He made some the ordinary remarks that Generals say to their troops and then made some promises that Jake knew he could not keep. Jake impulsively and emphatically stated, "General, you cannot do that!" The General gave Jake a funny look and replied, "Captain, you're right!" and he left. The others left behind in the club roared with laughter. They all thought Jake would really be in trouble in spite of the General's admission. Three weeks later, Jake was transferred to that General's headquarters. Since neither his superior officer nor Jake asked for the transfer, Jake was nervous. It seemed evident that everyone in his new assigned section had heard the story of Jake's big mouth and tensely waited for the axe to fall. Jake's immediate boss was a Major from Arkansas and they got along well, not like the other Arkansan that gave him a bad time in Korea. Jake started out making training inspections and ran into General Costello fairly frequently, as he would rather be out in the field than in his office. Never once did he mention Jake's telling him he could not keep his promises. Eventually, the General began to call Jake into his office to give him assignments regarding things the senior officer had a special interest in. Those assignments became so regular that it became embarrassing for Jake that Jake was in his office so much. But Major Files just laughed and would say, "I'm glad it's you and not me." The General had a reputation for being hard-nosed and almost everyone was afraid of him. Jake found out the hard way that day in the club that if a man stood his ground with the General and he was right then the soldier had nothing to worry about. However, Jake decided to be very careful in the future of how he spoke to a General, even if he came into a meeting unannounced.

After a couple months in Fort Jackson Jake began to do research on how he could get custody of his son. He worried about Edward; his stability, his security. He called every couple weeks to the house on 9th Avenue and brainstormed with Dorothy about her opinion of getting his son. Dorothy never seemed to be encouraging because she knew her daughter. Virginia had divorced her engineer husband and, not one to waste time, had remarried. Dorothy liked the new hubby, but now she had three grandchildren to worry about.

Edward was in 5th grade and back with his mom and his little sister, Liz, and his little brother, Bobby. They lived in San Diego and Eddie seemed to be doing alright. Jake knew that Dorothy spoiled the kid, but figured he needed it. He surely would not be spoiled at his mother's house although Eddie did get to go with his mom to Tijuana, Mexico now and then where Virginia sold insurance. Eddie loved it; the tacos, donkey rides, mom's attention. These trips neither Grandma Dorothy nor Jake approved of. Dorothy did not want Jake to get his hopes up and promised to do what she could to help him. Still, he waited for the day he would have Edward fulltime, if ever.

Life at Fort Jackson went on but the task changed. Jake felt this was one of the most important tasks of his Army career; revising all the five training manuals which were used to conduct the preparing of the trainees for assignment to regular Army units. The trainers were judged solely on the quality of the men that they put out, and the trainers, including the General, were proud of their product. So the quality of the guidance which they provided their trainers was critical. So after days and days of research, talking with the people conducting the training and meeting with people from the Infantry School at Fort Benning, Jake and his Sergeant that worked with him, finally completed a first draft. Then came days of trying to gain a consensus, which was more difficult than the writing. Finally, they were ready and they briefed everyone that they knew that had an interest in the new manuals, to come put their two cents worth in at a meeting. Judging from the number of people that showed up, invited and otherwise, lots of people wanted to put in their last word. Jake succeeded in getting the manuals published with lots of congratulations on his good work. He could never say he didn't publish a book; he published five! It was exhausting. He took a week off to get some rest!

Jake's life calmed down and his home life was peaceful. The Jacobs' couple had cozied into their military living, attended and hosted dinners with other couples, Alice painted, Jake racked up a few more university credits. But then, a directive came down from Washington DC to ship 200 men, a Captain, and a lieutenant to the 25th Division in Hawaii. Washington was to approve the selection. Jake's company submitted names twice and they were rejected, so Jake told Major Files that he was going to submit his own name as time was running out for the departure date. Jake did it and two weeks later he was on his way to Hawaii with Alice on her own way by car to San Francisco to ship the Chrysler, their belongings and herself to the Islands.

Chapter 18 ---- Aloha!

On July 15, 1957, Jake was bound for Schofield Barracks, Hawaii along with 200 soldiers. Traveling on two charter aircraft, they stopped in Oklahoma City, changed planes with another stop in Oakland, California to change planes again that would eventually take them to Honolulu. However, Jake realized during the Oakland changeover that the personnel records had not been transferred from the first airplane in Oklahoma City. Jake held up the Honolulu flight until the records were found and put on an airplane to be shipped immediately. The trip to Hawaii from that point on was uneventful, but the flight caused Jake time to reminisce about his past experiences in Hawaii; the stopovers on the USS Chaumont coming and going to China on his first assignment as a Marine, his scouting and bombing missions and trainings with his SB2C called "Dixie", and the stopover after watching the mushroom cloud from the atomic bomb that hit Hiroshima. So many memories flew in his mind, of which, most were pleasant. As he promised himself, he would not dwell on past negatives, only the good! It worked and he was looking forward to working and living a couple years on the beautiful island of O'ahu.

As the two aircrafts landed safely in Hawaii, Jake led his troops to their final destination, Schofield Barracks, located about 6 miles from the town, Wahiawa. In a valley between two volcanic mountains, this base was inland. The Kolekole

Pass was the destination for physical training runs by soldiers and, historically, the pass from which the Japanese Kamikaze pilots flew through to aid in the surprise attack on Pearl Harbor on that fateful December 7th day of 1941. Schofield Barracks, a training facility for the U.S. Army, boasts large open areas allowing for air assault operations to take off and land, a range control office, numerous semi-automated and other firing ranges, an Olympic size swimming pool along with barracks, enlisted housing and family housing sections.

As Jake found his officer quarters and settled down for his first night in Schofield Barracks, he was thankful the personnel records arrived as he and his troops did. What a flap there would have been if he had lost them! That would not be a good way to start out on his new assignment. The next morning the troops were split up among various units and Jake was assigned to the 1st Battle Group, 14th Infantry. Again he ended up in a staff position as the assistant S3, Plans & Operations. As described in the official Campaign Planning Handbook, his job would include designing and planning synchronized efforts and sequenced related operations to achieve a strategy for battle. This took someone who could envision the purpose and direction of military operations in many different areas. These strategies were designed to be able to execute campaigns that accomplished the nation's strategic objectives through the use of focused military force. Jake was part of that team of training troops at Schofield Barracks. That was his job. He was hand chosen for it and he would continue to be diligent and focused.

After checking Jake's military personnel records, the commanding officer decided that he was to prepare the forthcoming training tests which would be designed to test the capabilities of the Battle Group Officers. They had a tight schedule; military tight! The terrain on which they were to operate was totally unfamiliar to Jake so he spent the first few days out in the field analyzing the area on which he had to plan the tests. Alice was still on the ship with their belongings, but he was glad he was alone for there was very little time for sleep or settling in. Even when Alice arrived he knew she would have to take full responsibility for the preparations of the home front. Fortunately for Jake, he had a proficient clerk assigned to him for he prepared working drafts as fast as Jake could get them to him. His clerk would then have the drafts reviewed by his commanding officer, have them edited, (basically marked up) and on Jake's desk when he stopped by in the morning on his way out again. With Jake's usual efficiency the training tests were prepared and ready to go a week before they were due! Next was preparing and readying orders to be distributed to the participating units when they were being briefed. The tests were important for the careers of the officers; performance was everything. The mission was to always train for it was expected that the battle group could be deployed to the Far East at anytime. The Cold War was in full swing now; our nation had to be ready for what may or may not happen next!

Jake must have done a decent job for after just a few months in his Hawaiian assignment, Commander Colonel

Johnson decided to make him the Intelligence Officer of the Battle Group, making Jake the only Captain as the head of a staff section. The position usually called for a Major. Jake believed there was some envy amongst the officers, but as Jake rationalized, "That is life." An Intelligence Officer's responsibility was to collect information and analyze approaches to provide guidance and direction to commanders in support of their decisions so Jake's position varied; assessment of data and direction or response to questions as part of operation and campaign planning. These are based on the commander's information requirements which must be identified prior to the data collection and response. For example, intelligence is focused on supporting operations to the battle group such as briefings on current threats, sentiments of the local population, battlefield terrain, or movement of personnel or vehicles. Jake was sure he secured the position because of his analytical abilities and personal intelligence. He knew his thinking and confidentiality would eventually pay off! It did!

Even with very little time to sleep, Jake welcomed Alice to Hawaii and introduced her to their rented apartment in Honolulu just two blocks from the beach. Living like a tourist was very nice for a while since they were waiting for the new construction of the quarters at Schofield Barracks to be completed. The 25 mile drive to the office and home again took a toll on Jake; time was precious due to the strict military schedule he had to keep up. Alice understood, after all, she was able to enjoy the ocean and tourist atmosphere for many more hours than Jake. She felt this assignment for Jake was a real treat. She liked it. She decided to enjoy it as long as she could, plus she also knew that Jake was trying to get custody of his son. She had mixed feelings about that; jealousy, understanding, lack of control. Many emotions enveloped her, but she loved Jake and had known from the beginning of their marriage that some day she would be an active Step Mother. Not being a kid or animal person per se, Alice decided to make sure Jake understood what circumstances she would live under with a kid underfoot. Jake had agreed, since he would be out of town on business many times, she would have to take the bulk of parenting. She liked military living. She liked rules. She liked to enforce them. Just ask Jake. There were times she became upset with him after breaking a little rule such as not liking something she had cooked. He had learned, with Alice, it was easier and more peaceful to just do what she asked him to do. She was definitely the commanding officer in the house. Jake just wanted a chance to be with his son. He was getting the sense from Dorothy on 9th Avenue that it may be sooner than later, but he had to continue to be patient.

The new construction completed, Alice and Jake moved into their four-plex new housing with three bedrooms upstairs and the kitchen and living room down. It was delightful and Alice made it home with their furnishings, her paintings, and the Chrysler in the driveway. Jake even spent one Saturday morning planting banana trees in his yard with great hopes of eating a freshly picked banana each morning on his way to the office, which was only a few minutes walk away. When there was time he even walked home for lunch. In Jake's job assignment, he continued to get all sorts of odd jobs that Hank, his superior officer, would give him. He and Hank thought alike in many ways and when Hank wanted to get away from the phone, he and his wife would go to Jake and Alice's place. Alice liked to entertain and she did a good job of it; when it was on her terms. At any rate, lots of military work was accomplished during those evenings. There just never seemed to be enough time to do the job they were assigned to do. But, life was good! It got better, for awhile.

Life on 9th Avenue was challenging for Dorothy. She never minded a challenge, in fact, she liked to stay active mentally and socially. However, some of the challenges were certainly not her choice; they were her daughter's. Dorothy loved her grandchildren more than anything or one in her life. Eddie got the brunt of the lack of parenting from his mother, although, Liz and Bobby did not fair very well either. Poor Bobby had asthma and was a pistol of a little boy; much more energetic and unfocused than Eddie. Liz just wanted attention. During Eddie's fifth grade year, as he lived in San Diego with his Mom and Louis, he babysat not only his siblings, but his mother. She would come home from work, have a Martini, pat the kids on the head and rest. For being an engaging, friendly, intelligent woman who was able to secure a good paying, high esteem job, she sure did not know anything about mothering. Thank God she had a maid and a part time Nanny; and Eddie! Eddie would wait on his mom trying to capture her attention and approval. He would sit with her and watch movies, something they both treasured. When she said to Eddie about her drink, "This needs a little more kick in it," her son would run to the vodka bottle and pour some more kick in it. She obviously had a little drinking problem; but never one that stopped her from working. Virginia truly loved her children. She just was not nurturing. With all this going on, Dorothy had to nurture and monitor her grandchildren and sometimes that was a very tiring thing to do for a woman in her 60's. Even so, she once again took Eddie to her house to live for his 6th grade year. Now, most everyone understands a 6th grader is a very special beast; hormones are beginning to kick in, whatever manners they learned previously seem to dissipate, and caregivers want to pull their hair out. This is true whether that 6th grader is a boy or a girl. However, Grandma still took in her beloved Eddie and although he was a well mannered young man, he did have his moments. Dorothy also knew a young man needs a male role model. Herbie was it. Herbie cooked all the food. He liked to please Eddie so he cooked whatever he wanted. Plus, the two of them would sit out on the 9th Avenue porch and listen to Dodger games on the radio with Grandpa Herbie explaining the game as it went. Sometimes Dorothy would drive them to Dodger stadium where Grandpa Herbie and Eddie would eat peanuts and throw the shells on the ground while Eddie adorned his baseball glove ready to catch a foul ball. Eddie fell in love with the Dodgers; what was to become a life time passion. Eddie was happy. He was always happy living with his Grandma Dorothy and his Grandpa Herbie, and that is why, when his Grandma told him he was going to go visit his father, he worried a little. He should have worried a lot, because his life was about to take a 180 degree turn.

Back in Hawaii, Jake continued with his military schedule, always training whether it was locally at Schofield or on the Big Island of Hawaii. He would take his battle group to the Big Island where there was a huge training area. Again, he would have to prepare or help prepare plans for the training exercises plus serve as an umpire judging performances. There were times they would be there for a couple months at a time with only brief visits back to O'ahu and Alice. Sometimes Jake would remain at Schofield with intermittent training on the Big Island. Jake always seemed to have variation as he even worked in another capacity as a member of the 25th Division Brigade. This brigade had only a staff but no troop units. Troops were assigned to staff depending upon the task which was given them to perform. The brigade was commanded by a one star General named Manhart; a very accomplished and likeable person. With him on board, Jake and the other officers were able to procure much needed equipment and vehicles for it was expected for them to be prepared for deployment on a moment's notice. Once again, a Cold War could become a hot one at anytime and the military must be ready! It was a continuous rehearsal of "what ifs". Jake was responsible for evaluating his old unit the 14th Infantry as well as the other two battle groups in the division, the 19th and 22nd. The training area was located in the area between the mountains, Mona Loa and Mona Kea on the Big Island. Mona Loa, being the highest, seemed strange to have snow almost year round. This was Hawaii for heaven's sake! The terrain was all lava and covered with a fine powdered dust. When the troops were out in the dust working and training they would soon look like gray ghosts. A shower was always the first order of business when the training was completed. But, to Jake, there were pluses to this assignment, as he was always looking at the bright side of things. First, because the unit had planes and helicopters, they would do some sightseeing from the air capturing some great aerial pictures of an erupting volcano from directly above it. Another plus was that they made a deal with prisoners at the state prison. The prisoners grew flower gardens so all the wives of the unit would receive a huge arrangement of flowers on a weekly basis which was sent back on one of the daily courier flights. It never hurts to spoil the wife! And, at this point, Jake knew Alice needed some major spoiling, for things were about to change on the home front!

While spending more and more time on the Big Island, the news that Jake was getting visitors from California, specifically Dorothy and his son, he negotiated with the General for more time at Schofield Barracks as to not miss a moment with Edward. Dorothy who was not one to miss a chance for a leisurely, adventurous vacation, boarded a cruise ship with Eddie for a five day sail to Hawaii. What Dorothy did not expect, was her gall bladder attack; surely brought on by her anxiety over Eddie going to live with his father without the knowledge of that yet, Herbie being sick with cancer which Eddie did not know about, and her plight of what to do with her daughter's other two children who she needed to protect. Although Dorothy was miserable and confined to the ship's hospital for three nights, Eddie, a little worried about his Grandma, was entertained by the crew and had a delightful time! Why not? After all, he had just finished 6th grade! He was able to burn off energy and it was an adventure. Typical middle schooler! With relief that Grandma was well again, Eddie did not fully comprehend it when she told him his visit would be at least for one year! No wonder Lizzy, his sister, was crying at the docks as they boarded the ship. No wonder Eddie had a deep sense of worry. No wonder. But, as Grandma explained, it was time for his father to be in his life even if it meant Alice too. Dorothy was not too impressed with Alice, but she still deeply believed Eddie needed his Dad. And, even through Eddie's tears, it was to be!

After a week's stay in Honolulu, Grandma Dorothy boarded a cruise ship back to California to continue her charity work, her caring for her ill husband, and her protection of her other two grandchildren. It was August and the little family of three left behind at Schofield Barracks nestled into their newly constructed quarters. Jake was ecstatic and a little scared about having his son for two reasons; Alice's attitude and the fact that Edward's safety, education, and well being was now in his hands. With Alice's rules and schedules in place, Edward found as much time as he could to spend with his dad. He liked the ocean and the climate; always a nice feeling of warmth and when it rained, it was still warm. Hawaii. Nice place! He made friends on the base and followed the rules Alice set. He was afraid not to. She was not a warm person. His mom wasn't nurturing either, but she wasn't mean and she hugged him now and then. He did not want Alice to hug him. She was very intimidating and not very nice looking. Maybe it was her scowl, her barking orders, her demeaning way she talked to him and his father. He wanted to go home to Grandma, but he could not. He did love being with his gentle, soft spoken father even though he was firm, he was always fair. And school started. Every week day morning he and the other military children would board the Army bus and ride to Lailehua School, then a 7-12 public education facility. He made friends and Jake, as well as Edward, became more satisfied. Jake enrolled Edward into Pop Warner Football. He was a fast runner, just like his Dad but struggled with his Running Back position. As the season went on Edward became better and better and Dad became prouder and prouder. The season ended with Edward being quite successful and Jake happy he could get so much time off base to go to his games. Although Edward enjoyed the camaraderie of his team and the game itself, he missed baseball. Alice didn't care. She had plans for him and it did not include football or baseball. In fact, ball was not in the name at all. Swimming! In all fairness to Alice, each U.S. Army soldier and his children at Schofield Barracks were required to learn to swim. That meant Edward.

The General Robert Richardson Pool, Schofield Barracks, Hawaii was commissioned during World War II. The pool fulfilled the General's dream of "every soldier a swimmer." It was built as an Olympic training pool measuring 103 meters long and 25 meters wide with a training platform for diving. Hopes were that one day the Olympics could be held in Hawaii with Schofield hosting the swimming. That never happened although it was used as a practice pool in 1972 for the US Olympic Diving team prior to going to Munich, Germany. The pool was constructed to meet all required international specifications for competition. The pool produced world ranking swimmers and diving teams largely due to the fact that the quality of Hawaiian swimmers heading home after the war and the Army's willingness to promote training and competition of national competitors. The pool had always been used to teach every soldier to swim, to teach combat swimming to save lives as well as used for recreational swimming. That was what Edward wanted to do, swim recreationally, but that was not to be. On January 2, 1959 he began his swim lessons instructed by two of the leading swim coaches in the United States: Hawaiian natives, Buddy Amina and Bill Woolsey. Bill Woolsey won the Gold Medal in the 800 meter freestyle in 1952, Helsinki Olympics. Then in 1956 he earned the Silver Medal in the same event in the Melbourne Olympic games. And as coaches, they were both great. Not wanting to have any part in this so called "sport" Edward balked and whined which went nowhere with Alice or his father. However, within a month he had learned to swim and proceeded to the next level. He was good at that swimming sport. Was it agility, his athletic ability, or was he so angry at his having to live with such a barbaric step mother that he became so fast; and outstanding? It felt good to win. Edward had not felt he was a winner since he played baseball in the vacant field with the high school boys during his 6th grade year. The teenagers would knock on his Grandma's door, ask if Eddie could come and play ball, and off he would go. He was a winner on that field and in Hawaii. He had become a winner again! He also had a person he admired and who helped his self esteem more than anyone else, Coach Amina. He would expect Edward to do his best, swim his hardest, but he always gave him compliments. If Edward was having a bad day and he was down in the dumps, Coach Amina knew how to get him feeling better. He was a good listener, a great mentor. So, of course, Edward wanted to please him. As a swimmer for the Schofield Shark Swim Club, Edward practiced a lot. In less than a year, he was the Hawaiian record holder in the 100 meter backstroke in his age group, 12 years. Unfortunately, his father had missed that meet for he was on the Big Island training and preparing troops for combat; but he would never forget that weekend when the General called him from Schofield and asked, "Do you know what your son did today?" Jake was a little nervous. He knew Edward was a good boy, but one never knows what a boy might do, so he answered timidly, "No, what?" "He broke the Hawaiian swim record for the 100 meter backstroke in his age group, 12 years old. He is now a Hawaiian record holder!" Jake puffed up with pride, but because he believed in being a model of value by example and precept, he said thank you and called home to speak to his son, the record holder. Go figure! Good for him! Must take after his Pa after all. Alice did not seem as puffed up, only driven. That win seemed to motivate her to stand over Edward at the pool during practices to scream at him and make him work harder, harder, harder. Break the record, again, again, again. It was exhausting not to mention embarrassing and demeaning to the victim of her affliction, Edward. Coach Amina, who quickly tired of her tormenting, demanded Alice to stay away from the pool when her step son was practicing or racing. She was not welcome. She could watch from the stands, but no interruptions in the future were allowed. Jake was also called to support the coach on this, and in fact, the General was also informed. Alice had been banned from the pool. Edward was relieved, at first. But there would be hell to pay at home!

Edward's record stood for many years and he set new records in the 13-14 year old categories. Jake truly believed Edward's successful swimming experience was a turning point in his son's life; he learned discipline was not only exercised by parents and coaches but by oneself. Unfortunately, to Jake's dismay, Alice continued her abusive attitude towards his son. When Alice took Edward home the day she was kicked out of the pool, he was hit with a yardstick many times. Alice continued her abusive, demeaning attitude toward Edward whenever Jake was away for a few days; she tamed it when Jake was around. Jake knew what was going on and many times would take his son outside to counsel him on how to live with Alice. "I know she can be quite hard to live with, just do what she wants and you will be okay. I really do understand." Edward loved his father with all his heart so he did his best to be like his father and follow all of Alice's rules. He ate his food that Alice had prepared most of the time. He went to school and got A's in most of his classes. He swam hard and won lots. However, his hormones were raging and at times so was his temper. Unable to always bite his tongue, like his father did, he would lash out. Big mistake. Alice would beat him with the oak yardstick, force his uneaten food down him by mixing it all up in a blender and leaving him to drink it. One very bad mixture of food included sardines. Edward could not and would not drink it. Another oak yardstick pounding. She made sure Edward felt it was all his fault, he was the cause of the abuse. She also let him know that she was mean telling him of the times she, as a girl, would tie her horses tail to a fence and beat it. Who does that stuff? She would tell him he was lazy, spoiled, stupid although she had only a 6th grade education and he was getting straight A's. But, it worked. Edward took the blame and his self esteem, what he had of it, plummeted. He did not complain to his father. What good would that do? But Jake knew about it. He lived it! But Jake also knew if he pushed Alice too far, he would have to send Edward back to California and he could not bear losing him again. He, having his own abandonment issues with women, could not allow the loss of Alice either; so everyone had to go on with Jake trying to calm everyone down when he was at Schofield Barracks. One of the ways he did that was by taking Edward on drives, just he and him, in his new Borgward Isabella stationwagon. It was German made and built like a tank, just like a Chrysler. One day as they were touring the island together they came upon an avocado tree located on the grounds of the local Catholic Church. Jake loved avocadoes so he made a deal with his son. "Edward, you climb the tree, I will shake it, and we will both pick up the avocadoes that drop off." They did! Edward found it to be quite the adventure and it also told him something about his dad; although he followed all rules military style, he still had a little bit of mischief and fun in him. It gave Edward and Jake a great deal of bonding.

One morning Jake's neighbor, Dr. Taft, came to the Jacobs' door excited for Jake and Edward to see his new sailboat sitting in his driveway. They all admired the small boat, capacity of four people. In a moment's notice, Dr. Taft, Jake, and Edward were dressed in casual shorts and in the car with boat being towed behind heading for the Waikiki Harbor boat dock launching ramp. After getting it into the Pacific, Jake was dumbfounded to find out that Dr. Taft had no idea how to sail a boat. Neither did Jake nor Edward. They might have been okay, except for the fact it was low tide and the reef just beyond the docks was exposed. As the little boat headed for the reef, no one in the boat could maneuver it away. Crunch! Yes, the boat hit the reef and there it sat, stuck! The waves splashed against it, but it would not budge. Edward, being the super swimmer, begged to swim to shore to get help; it could not have been more than 2 miles or so. The two men decided that could be dangerous for the boy, so they waited for the Coast Guard to come and save them. Humiliating, yes! Funny, yes! Memorable, absolutely! Did they go sailing again, no! Dr. Taft sold his boat with a hole in it.

Then came Hawaii's Statehood on August 21, 1959. Celebrations exploded throughout the islands. There were parades, festivals, American flags, and severe storms. It was the worst and harshest storm season on record. There was storm after storm. The native Hawaiians believed it was because the spirits were angry. Native Hawaiians embraced community and heritage above personal gain, so many were not happy about Hawaii becoming a state. Many were not surprised when hurricane warnings were constant but the big one during that season was Hurricane Dot, just before the official statehood date. Occurring from August 1-8, Hawaii was hit hard by Dot, a category 4 hurricane. It came into O'ahu in full fury. Schofield Barracks, being inland, knew it would get the high winds but fortunately, the 35 foot waves would not impact them. Everyone had to hunker down when it hit Schofield on August 6th! Jake and his family stayed on the bottom floor of their home, stayed away from the windows, kept their flashlights near, and listened to their battery powered radio to track the progression of the storm. Finally, when the storm had passed, the damage was enormous, but no one on the base was hurt or killed. The storm had gusts of up to 65 mph which was not as high as the 125 on other islands, but the local flooding from torrential rains was substantial. On Hawaii and Oahu there was an estimated property damage of no more than $150,000, not bad. However, the damage to agriculture cost over 6 million dollars, devastating! Jake wondered the next day if that estimate included his banana trees; they were ruined! Jake was not happy. He cheered himself up once again by not dwelling on his bananas, but rather on how lucky they all were to get so little damage and no lives lost. He and Edward also thought it was ironic that the Hurricane's name was Dot, short for Dorothy! The Native Hawaiians had their theory about the storm, and so did the Jacobs' boys!

1959 was a long year for Edward and for Jake also. He loved having his son with him, but he was gone a lot, missing out on many of Edward's accomplishments and downtimes. He was very attentive to Edward when he was home; probably causing Alice some jealousy issues. However, Jake did what he felt he had to do, be an example for his son and make him strong. Jake understood that Edward came to him on the spoiled side. Even more reason for him to be with his father, which Dorothy also recognized. He did not like how Alice treated him, but he also knew Alice was teaching him some good life skills; perseverance, obedience to authority, self discipline. Granted, Edward had a lot of that already from his father, but a child needs to be trained. And trained he became. Not happy, but what middle school kid is truly happy with the situation at home? Or so Jake rationalized.

In October, Jake received a disturbing and sad phone call from Dorothy. Herbie had died two days after the Dodgers won the World Series. She, of course, was distraught and knew Eddie would be too. His Grandpa Herbie had cancer and that was one of the reasons she decided Eddie should be with his father because Herbie, who Eddie loved so much, was getting very ill and she knew it would not be long before he died. Eddie, who loved his Dodgers almost as much as Herbie did, would appreciate the fact they won the big one so his Grandpa could rest in peace. Jake remembered his promise to himself about crying, but when he broke the news to Eddie, they both cried. As Jake said, "I liked Herbie. He was a good man." Now, more than ever, Jake had to step up to the plate and somehow replace Herbie which he knew he could never do.

February of 1960, Dorothy and her sister Claire, arrived in Hawaii for a vacation and of course to see Eddie. Eddie was beside himself with delight. He demonstrated his swimming abilities, showed off his trophies, introduced Grandma to his coaches, ate ice cream and was showered with hugs. It was truly a beautiful time for Grandma and grandson. Not so much for Alice who was steaming with jealousy and the feeling of loss of control; but she behaved nicely because she knew the power of Dorothy and how Jake wanted to keep his son. One evening Jake decided to take the visitors out to dinner in a lovely restaurant on Waikiki Beach. The view from the table was breathtaking of the Pacific Ocean. Edward was dressed up with slacks, dress shirt and a tie; everyone thought he was so handsome, including the other cliental in the restaurant. Father, Step Mom, Grandma and Aunt shone with pride! Yes sir, that child belonged to them. Things went well until too much alcohol passed the lips of Dorothy and Alice. The argument began quietly and then escalated ending outside in a fist fight. What caused the fight? Booze and Eddie of course. Alice had started it with the comment about the spoilt child; Grandma responded like a Grizzly Bear protecting her young. Jake and Edward escaped most of the humiliation of the public display of a cat fight by Jake paying the bill and quietly sneaking outside to take a walk on the beach; just the two sane males.

Jake and Alice argued. That was unusual. Jake was not a man to argue or yell. But he did! Alice liked Hawaii. She liked having control of her men. She did not want to go back to the mainland, but Jake would not agree to another year in Hawaii when he was exhausted from his responsibilities of his military assignment and he knew he had only temporary custody of Edward so he would have to send him back to California. He would not let that happen! Even if Alice was unhappy. Too bad. This time Edward and Jake won. So, in May 1960, the Jacobs' packed up their house and drove their German Borgward to Honolulu to stay in a motel until their transport to the mainland of the United States arrived. The second day into the wait, Alice and Jake decided to leave Edward in the motel and go to dinner alone just a couple blocks away. He was almost 14 years old, so staying alone was okay with him. Jake grabbed him a pizza and coke from the nearby pizza place and left Edward happily munching away and watching TV. Although there was a storm warning, Jake was not concerned. It was just a warning, so no problem, they were only a couple minutes away. As Alice and Jake had a peaceful, last Hawaiian dinner together the storm warning turned into tsunami watches. They also ignored that but watched the ocean as they ate. As the winds increased so did the waves and so did the rainfall. Jake could not remember if it was the huge wave he saw first or the siren blaring, but he threw money at the waiter and began running back to the motel in fear for his son. Alice, perturbed that her husband should dessert her in such a way, decided to trot after him. Fortunately, the wave did not hit hard, the winds died down and they all made their transport the next day to the mainland with no incident. Once again Alice learned, don't mess with Jake when he fears for his son. How much longer must she endure this?

Chapter 19 -- Seattle – The Final Assignment

Abusers have a fine art of manipulating the emotions of the abused so the blame is on the victim not the abuser. Secrets are kept that way. No one who blames themselves for all the misery they have caused will tell others about what happens to them as punishment. They deserve to be abused, after all, they have only themselves to blame. Alice had this down pat. She had control over Edward and her husband. Both blamed themselves for their rightful abuse. And if either told anyone, even each other, there would be more pain. They were made to believe they would suffer more, if they told a soul. No one would want them and love them then. And so, life went on as Jake was assigned to Fort Lawton located in Seattle, Washington.

An uneventful military transport flight for Alice and Edward ended in San Francisco, a couple days at the Presidio, then off to stay with friends near the military facility of Travis Air Force Base. Jake caught up to them there as they proceeded by car, the Borgward of course, to Olympia, Washington's courthouse for the most important hearing of father and son's life; to get full custody of Edward. Virginia, Dorothy, Alice, Edward and Jake gathered before the judge with great nervousness and hope. As the judge heard everyone's, including Alice's, reason why Edward should live with them, the judge took 14 year old Edward into his chambers and asked one of the most life changing questions of the teenager's life, "With whom do you want to live?" Edward, having already thought this out knowing this court hearing was coming up answered, "My Dad". The judge of course asked, "Why?" Edward replied, "Because I love him, respect him, and I want to be with him." Jake had promised not to shed a tear again about

anything, so when he heard the judge's decision, "Full custody goes to Nelson Edward Jacobs" he kept his promise to himself; but he wanted to cry. He was so relieved and happy. And Alice, irritably realized she had to endure that kid a while longer! Dorothy was actually relieved with this decision for her belief remained firm that he needed his father, so as she hugged Edward goodbye she gave him what would later be one of his greatest joys, a small transistor radio. Dorothy knew he could listen to his Dodgers with it. She also was thankful her Eddie would be able to visit her periodically. She had missed her first grandson.

After the custody hearing, Eddie joyfully joined his mother and grandmother in his mom's Chrysler and headed South on the I-5 while Alice and Jake piled into their Borgward to travel North on the I-5. Eddie was to enjoy a two week hiatus from Alice to visit his mother, grandmother and siblings. Jake and Alice stopped in Tacoma to sell their first house, bought a newly constructed house in Newport Hills in Bellevue, Washington and Jake reported into Fort Lawton to begin his assignment as the officer in charge of the Western ROTC programs in Oregon, Washington, Idaho, Utah, Montana, and Wyoming. Reserve Officers'

Training Corps, ROTC, was, and still is, a group of college based officer training programs that train young men and women to become commissioned officers of the United States Armed Forces. Army ROTC students are called cadets, are trained in military assault, warfare, strategies, physical preparedness, leadership, and, after graduation, have an active duty obligation to the U.S. Military. Being his last military assignment, it was perfect for Jake for his experience in the military was training, management, evaluations, and piloting. That was probably the most exciting thing for Jake, the piloting. Having a current pilot license, he was assigned a small military plane with a "co-pilot" where he personally transported himself to the ROTC universities to monitor and manage the training of the students. The job suited him. On April 12, 1961 he was promoted from Captain to Major by order of the Secretary of the Army. That pleased him. His ability to work well with people and his quiet sense of humor went well with working with university Board of Directors and Presidents. He met Joe Albertson one meeting at the University of Idaho. He often reflected on that meeting; 'ole Joe was a likeable, honest fellow. He promised himself wherever there was an Albertson's store, he would shop there. He told Alice that was the super market for her. She actually agreed to that. She liked Albertsons. And secretly, Jake liked his job that meant being away from home for a couple days a week. Edward would be active in high school and swimming practice; he would be okay!

The six weeks Eddie was in California was a peaceful

time for Alice and for Jake too! Busily setting up their new home, acclimating themselves to their new community, assimilating to Jake's new assignment, and no Edward to look after. Once again Alice seemed calmer and loving to Jake; however, she was steaming inside. How dare that kid stay six weeks with his Grandmother. He was supposed to be back in 2-3 weeks, but Jake allowed him to stay there when Dorothy called him and begged. He told her to have him back one week before school started. It began on the day after Labor Day. Alice had things that needed to be done; registration of school, and an entire list of chores. Besides, how dare he go and enjoy life. That kid needed discipline, her discipline. Of course, Jake had his own ways of discipline for Edward, not that he was in charge of that in his home. However, Jake believed his son needed toughening up and, being a military trainer, he established an exercise program for Edward that included daily pushups and a couple mile run. Edward was going to be very busy when he got home.

The public schools in Hawaii were not rated very well and Jake would have to agree with the rating. It really was no fault of the administration or the teachers; most students were Native Hawaiian and the education level at home was not very high causing attitudes about education to not be conducive to learning. Many of the Natives believed in a more spiritual, nature driven education and the belief of labor for the good of the community, not for self promotion. The Hawaiian language was used throughout the islands in homes as well as the community. Formal education in the public schools required English skills. The result was Pigeon English; the mixture of English and Hawaiian. Since schools were, and still are today, rated on their National test scores, Hawaii came in at a rate of 50; the lowest of all the states. That is why Jake had decided "if" he was going to stay in Hawaii for another tour in the Army, Edward would had gone to Punahou School, the private K-12 school that required entrance exams, proficiency in English, and a truck load of cash as tuition. Once Jake finally got Edward back to him from California via a United Airlines flight and a late night pick up, Edward was enrolled in the local middle school, Tyee Junior High. Jake had sent Alice to enroll Edward. As she filled out the paperwork and handed Edward's 7th and 8th grade transcripts over to the Vice Principal, she was astonished and dismayed to hear him explain that Edward would be enrolled in 8th grade, not 9th. He explained that any student having been educated in Hawaii would not be able to keep up with the vigorous curriculum that Tyee Middle School had to offer. After her surprise, her inner Alice kicked in! She became angry. Of course, anger from a parent only gets school administrators annoyed, so Alice had to become calm and logical instead. Bottom line came when she proposed Edward be enrolled in 9th grade and if his grades did not reflect his ability by the end of the first quarter, then she would be willing to let him go back to 8th. Good job Alice! More importantly, she actually fought for him. Her personal efforts and mothering of this child came into question as she sat in front of the Vice Principal and she would show him. She did. Edward did outstanding at school. She was not disappointed, but you would never had known it by her continued demeaning behavior towards him. She was still furious about how long he had stayed in California; he would pay. She did not speak to him for two months. It actually turned out quite well for Edward and Jake. It was peaceful. Edward went to school, did well, swam, did the chores expected of him and Jake flew to his various universities to check on the ROTC programs.

Freshman, sophomore, and junior years came and went with the same-o routine for everyone at the Jacobs' family. Jake enjoyed the Northwest. In fact, he loved it. The beautiful forests, Puget Sound, camaraderie at work, social functions with Alice, watching his son do well swimming and running track. He had even managed to train Edward; pushups and running. All this helped him with his endurance and ability in track and swimming. Jake would quietly and proudly go to his son's meets; watching "stone faced" from the top stands. In fact, Edward's friends would say to Edward, "Stone Face was in the stands today." That meant his dad. Jake rarely went down to congratulate him on a swim or a run nor did he bring it up at home. Now and then he would meet up with his only child after the meet and say, "That was a good run but maybe you could check with your coach on how to go a little faster." Jake felt the less said the better because Edward needed to be his own disciplinarian. Jake did not want to interfere. He knew the most well trained disciplined man does not need the trainer's approval, only his own. Although Edward was happy to know his dad was watching him, it would have gone a long way in his relationship with his son had Jake just now and then said how proud he was of Edward. Every son wants his dad's approval.

Sometimes Jake thought perhaps they were too hard on Edward. He would hear Alice belittling Edward after a Saturday of trimming the yard and mowing the lawn. Instead of saying thank you, Alice would always find a fault with the work and demand it to be redone or fixed. Nothing was ever good enough, not even Edward's grades. The best thing was that Edward spent very little time at home; he was the editor of the Sammamish High School newspaper, a track star, a record breaking swimmer and an accomplished student. Jake was as proud as any father could be; but being the self disciplined person he was, Jake never bragged. Jake had begun thinking perhaps he was a little hard on Edward when his good friend, neighbor and Superintendant of Schools frankly stated that Alice and Jake needed to lighten up on Edward. They were way too tough on him. He mentioned all the pushups, but also the three mile walk home after track and swim meets; usually in the cold and wet climate of the Northwest. That seemed a little too harsh. That was a little humiliating for Jake to hear, but although he became a little concerned, he did little about it; he watched his son grow and mature. Why rock the boat with Alice if Edward was progressing? What Jake didn't see was, when he was traveling, the dysfunctional way Alice treated his son. Sometimes, Edward would hear Alice walk into the bathroom while he was showering; why would she do that? That made it even more awkward for Edward being a young teenage male and very aware of himself becoming a man; Alice, also, was aware. Many a night after being emotionally abused and a few whaps of the oak yardstick against his buttocks, he would slip out his window and go into the green house next door. There Edward did not have to fear that Alice would come into his room and harass him. He slept there many a night and slipped back early in the morning through his cracked window to run in the rain to school early so there would be less time to spend at home with that mean spirited and demented woman. After awhile, Edward began to wonder where the little cot came from that was in the greenhouse. The house was owned and lived in by an older, very kind couple; they had never told Edward, but they knew he was sleeping there some nights and they were well aware of the harassment at home. They had called Jake and talked privately to him. Jake also knew another way Edward would sooth himself would be to listen to the Dodger game with his transistor radio. Since the Minor Dodger League was in Spokane, Edward could pick up the game from there. He would put the small radio under his pillow, put his ear to it, and laid in his bed at night listening to the game. Many times this was his salvation and escape from the real world of home. Jake never told Alice about these two escapes for his son; for she would have made things far worse for Edward. And for him!

In 1962 Jake's ROTC assignment turned to the

management of the inactivation of the Air Force at Fort Lawton while keeping the site under Army control. Through his previous military assignments, he was the man for the job. Long hours kept him at the base, but for only a few months, for on October 31, 1962 the Army Commendation Medal was given to him for his meritorious service from June 1, 1960 to October 31, 1962. The next day, November 1, 1962, he officially retired from the Army and became a civilian again.

Chapter 20 -- Civilian! Take 2!

With so much time on his hands as a retiree, Jake continued to keep his brain strong by going to the University of Washington extension classes in Bellevue, an easy way for Jake to chalk up more university hours; and a way to stay clear of Alice. What really captivated his attention was the real estate market. Why not become an agent, sell new constructed homes and buy one? Once Jake decided to accomplish a task, he did! With real estate license in hand, he secured a sales position at the new home subdivision of Newport Hills near Bellevue. Located at Phantom Lake, and within a mile and a half of Sammamish High School, Jake and Alice bought their new home just a block from the small beautiful, peaceful lake which was to become known as "the lake house". Unlike his sales job at B. F. Goodrich, Jake enjoyed the challenges and rewards of this sales position. Not only did he sell the homes, but he managed the sales which included supervision of the building of the home to match what the buyer paid for. He sold, managed paperwork, wrote reports and evaluated the progress of each individual home. He also was responsible for the operation of the model homes and grounds of the subdivision. Alice seemed to enjoy the new surroundings of her "lake house". She painted, kept the house meticulous, cooked, socialized with the wives of the men Jake met in the real estate business, and yet, was miserable.

Jake took orders. He finished tasks. He took pride in his work. No matter if it was the military, home, or a buyer. Jake accepted his lot in life. It fit him perfectly. What did not fit him was his feeling of lack of control with the discipline of his son. Edward was a very well disciplined young man at the age of 17 and a senior in high school. His competitive swimming, track and editor of the paper kept him busy and out of the house. When he was home, he obeyed all the rules and studied. Although he was proud of Edward, he felt he could not let up on him too much; however, he also knew Alice would not! Once again, Jake rationalized, "All teenagers are not happy about their home life. It is natural." Jake was right about that! Only about 15% of teens are happy with their relationships with parents. It is the time when they want freedom, a time to spread their wings. Most are sick of being told what to do. Unfortunately for the teens, they do not realize their brains and reasoning skills are still developing and guidelines are important to help them stay safe; thus, that is why God created parents. But then again, guidelines do not mean "abusive behavior".

One morning while walking the subdivision to monitor the home building progress of his buyers, Jake was jolted by the news of President John F. Kennedy's assassination. It was November 22, 1963, and the leaves were deep under his feet like a golden, orange layer of crisp snow. Shocked and saddened by this event, it clicked into Jake's memory of his son's sophomore year when Edward organized a 50 mile walk because JFK challenged all teens to be more physically active. Edward took the challenge and led dozens of other students to do their part. When Edward got back to the high school late that day after walking 50 miles, he called his parents to pick him up. Alice got the phone call. She told him to walk home; "another 3 miles won't kill you." It had become a rainy cold day. As Edward drug himself into the house an hour later, Jake was stunned. He had no idea. He would have picked him up. Shaking his head to rid himself of the memory of that day, he grieved for JFK and America. But that did not relieve the fact that Jake felt stuck in his relationship between Edward's needs and Alice's. It would not break loose. Until later.

Gone was the greenhouse escape, but Edward still had his transistor radio. Miraculously, Alice never found out about it or surely it would have been confiscated. Edward had found another escape, vanilla ice cream. He and his father loved their treat. When Alice let them, they each had one scoop after dinner. Jake would wink at his son as they were slowly savoring their favorite food. One scoop was not enough for Edward, so he concocted a brilliant plan to eat more ice cream. When the parents were in bed, he would grab his hidden spoon, sneak quietly into the garage where the freezer held the 2-gallon carton of ice cream, take it out, pry the bottom of the carton off, and dig in from the bottom up. Mmmmm! They never noticed. When it came to ice cream, he won!

Jake wondered why Alice was walking away from Edward's room with his son's box of baseball cards in her grasp. He knew Edward had one very prized possession and that was that box of cards. Jake realized how emotionally attached he was to the cards because most of them were collected when he walked with his Grandpa Herbie to the store. Herbie would buy Edward a pack each time, then the young boy would categorize them, memorize each player's stats and file them. Alice let Jake know she was storing them for his son so school work could be done! Jake was okay with that. What Jake never knew was one month later while he was at work, Alice grabbed the box of cards and Edward, drove to the local dump and had her stepson watch as she threw the box away! Edward was mortified. At age 16 ½ he cried when he got home. He had lost more than the cards, he felt he lost Grandpa Herbie for the second time.

Jake was aware of Edward leaving earlier than necessary to school by foot. He was a track guy; usually he ran. Sammamish High School was his safe haven. He busied himself with the editing of the paper, studying, running, swimming and with his girl, Valera Ann. It was a very 1960's boy-girl relationship; handholding, kissing, no sex. Not appropriate. Both of their parents would probably kill them if they even thought about sexual intercourse, so they didn't. They just enjoyed the school's activities together and her new Thunderbird. Edward had all his credits covered, so he decided to take a study hall during one period. When Alice got wind of that, she was irate. Of course, she was always irate, but this time it could be a "beating irate" if Edward wasn't careful, so Edward said he would sign up for another class. He did! It was Driver's Education. Why tell his parents about it? After all, what they did not know, would not hurt them. Or him, right? His swim coach, Mr. Stutz, just happened to be the instructor; no lucky coincidence. He knew it when he signed up. Learning to drive would serve him well in the future; even if it meant not until he went to college.

And college he prepared for! He better have. That was all Jake and Alice did; talk about what university Edward was going to go to. What? Edward's decision? No. Just study, keep up your good grades, swim, run, and get scholarships. He was accepted to Oregon State, Washington State, and, Jake's favorite, University of Washington. In February of his senior year, the State Congressman recommended Edward for an appointment to Annapolis. His father was ecstatic. Alice was smug. In her mind she felt it was a reflection on her terrific parenting and it would get Edward away from her; far away. The receiver of the recommendation did not share their feelings. In fact, he really did not have any real feelings about any of those schools, except, he would be on his own or at least, away from his wicked step mother. He knew his dad would love for him to go to Annapolis, so accepting his fate because he felt he had no choice, he went to Bremerton, Washington with a few other fellows with recommendations in the Seattle area, for a physical and academic testing. Taking the ferry back from Bremerton, Edward noticed he was picked up by his parents at the Seattle docks without a hassle. Lead a march for the president for 50 miles, you have to walk home in the rain; get a recommendation at a military school, you get good service. Okay, Edward gets it! He received high scores both physically and academically from the military screening and was set for an appointment. All he had to do was apply. It never happened. Too much interference preceded it!

Winter break arrived with opening of gifts with his father and Alice, then a delightful, loving car ride with Grandma Dorothy to Portland, Oregon, where his bank working mother, his two brothers and his sister lived with Louis, his step father. Two brothers you say? On March 18, 1962, Charlie was born to Virginia and Louis. Jake could not believe his ears. More children for Virginia? Does God not have any mercy? Of course, when Edward was picked up for the drive to Portland, Dorothy told the story of Virginia's reaction to the pregnancy. From San Diego, where she conceived Charlie, Virginia was on her way in a taxi to Mexico where she had planned to "get rid of it". Louis, Charlie's dad, got word of her plan and headed after the taxi in his car. Got there right in time; the taxi was in line to cross the border. As Louis swung the taxi door open he demanded Virginia to get out of the cab. She refused so he pulled her out and dragged her to his car where they went home. She had Charlie to Louis' delight. "Oh brother." thought Jake. Edward was excited to see his new brother and renew his relationship with his hyper, fun loving brother and his beautiful, ditzy sister. He stayed as long as he could in Portland with his family; playing, babysitting, relaxing, enjoying his life, and dreading going back. He did love his life at school. And swimming. He was doing very well in those areas. Finally, his father called to find out when he was coming home. Alice wanted him back immediately. Hard to understand that since she was the one who wanted him gone, permanently. Jake sent him a bus ticket. It arrived late at night in the local bus station. As Edward with his travel bag in hand, called home at the payphone, Alice responded by telling him to walk home. He knew the way, but the cold January 1st rain and wind was brutal. Nothing Edward could do about it, so he began his trek home. The distance was about 8 miles, over the Mercer Island Bridge, drudging along. Depressed. "Here I go again…but only until June 3, graduation day. Not too much longer…" After an hour and a half of walking, "Beep, beep". Edward looked up to see his father. He was picking him up to take him home. And they both had hell to pay for that!

Alice did not speak to Edward for at least three months. It was nice not to hear her voice; except some evenings he could hear her yelling at his Dad and in return, his Dad, always calm, trying to sooth her. Poor Dad. Why does he take it? Life went on and Edward was swimming more and more. The Tokyo, 1964, Olympics was coming up and he knew he could qualify in a couple events. So, with renewed energy and a goal he wanted to meet, he swam. He swam hard. And fast. He broke records in the 100 meter backstroke, 200 meter freestyle. He swam in the Sunset Public Pool in Beaverton, Oregon against Don Schollander, the rising star of the swim world. Edward beat him in both events. His father actually told him he was proud of his times. But, news came down that the events that Edward qualified in were cut from the Olympics in Tokyo in 1964. Disappointment, once again, overwhelmed Edward. But, he continued swimming. It helped him to focus his energy and anger; and kept him away from home. Schollander went on to win four gold medals including the events: 400 freestyle and 400 medley relay. His best event was the 200 meter freestyle, but it was not included in the 1964 Olympics. And Edward knew if it had been, Edward would have won the Gold. Jake was proud of his son, he just didn't tell him.

On May 4, 1964, with permission from his father, Edward and Valera Ann, adorned in formal attire were picked up by another Sammamish High School couple and driven to the high school gym for their Junior-Senior Prom. It was elegantly decorated and the local band played all the current '60's music. Eating cookies and fruit punch, the four students relaxed, danced, laughed. Knowing the curfew for all of them was midnight, they left the prom at 11 pm, leaving time for the biggest, sweetest, gooiest bowl of ice cream in town at the Dairy Queen. After dropping off Valera Ann, Edward was dropped off at the "lake house". Just to be sure he did not wake up anyone when he arrived home, he slipped through his bedroom window (always conveniently left open a crack, just in case…), got into his pajamas, and went to sleep. The time of hitting the pillow was exactly, 12:14 am. Ripped out of his sleep to the door being thrown open and a huge dark shadow of a person invading his room terrified Edward. It was

1:30 a.m. Jumping out of bed and pressing himself against the wall out of fear, he recognized Alice. This time she did not have an oak yard stick in her hand, no. She was wielding the fireplace poker! And screaming at him. "You are late! You were out screwing your pretty little girl friend! How dare you! You will pay for that!" The horrified teen was shocked. And then, the beating began. Over and over she hit his legs and his buttocks. He dare not yell out after the first hit; it seemed to get worse and worse and he knew he would surely die this time. It continued until Jake's calm, firm voice said, "That's enough Alice. Put it down." She backed off but it was too late for Edward. He crawled back into his bed, buried his head in his pillow and with no Dodger game available, he cried himself to sleep. What had he done wrong? Nothing. Only one more month, he would graduate, turn 18, and then free at last!

On Monday when he went to school he was careful to cover his swollen legs, his bruises, his cuts from the attack. Can't let anyone know. But Valera Ann caught on. After he broke down and told her, she immediately took him to her mother. Being a kind, good widow and having a brother who was a lawyer, she had no patience for this child abuse. She immediately called her sibling for legal counsel. He was on his way. She kept Edward with her until her brother arrived. He counseled him, took him to see the principal so all the nastiness of what had been happening in the household could be aired. The principal was horrified. He had no idea, and except for the few times Edward shared some times at home with his swim coach, neither did any of the teachers. Here was a very good student, star athlete, good citizen and he was being physically and emotionally abused at home. The police were called and Edward was taken to the local Juvenile Hall under protective custody until the next day. Alice and Jake were informed of the abuse charges, where their son was and the hearing the next morning. Grandma Dorothy and Virginia were called by the authorities and told that if they wanted any say about this teenager, they better be there in court the next day. They were. Edward appeared in court the next day aghast and more nervous than ever before in his life. As the judge brought Alice and Jake before the bench, they admitted to the abuse. Jake lost custody. Dorothy got it! Head down, shoulders bent, Jake left the courthouse not to hear from his son again for a long time. When he got home, he realized no longer was he stuck. He also realized he lost his son. He cried.

Edward finished his high school year at Sammamish living in a nearby motel with his Grandmother. He did not walk at his graduation. He said goodbye to Velara Ann and never followed up on any of the universities he was accepted into, including the application to Annapolis. He was tired. He was ready to go home with Grandma and find education in California. He was finished living with his father. He was worried about his father but he also knew the choice was his father's, not his. Goodbye Dad.

Chapter 21 – And Life Goes On.

It took Jake quite some time to overcome the humiliation of the court hearing and he, of course, never really got over losing the custody of his son. Long sleepless nights were spent contemplating his son's leaving home at 18; similar to him leaving Arkansas at 19. Both left on bad terms. He struggled inwardly with his philosophy of letting the past hurt go and to live for today, look to the future. At times it seemed to him he did not have a future, except with Alice to whom he was committed. He realized for the first time during his mourning process over his son, that he did not really love her much. But, he was afraid; of more severe emotional abuse from her and of losing her. What if she were gone? What would he do then? And, after all, he had defied her when he picked Edward up on that January 1st morning. He also had stopped her from killing him with a fireplace poker. For that she should have been grateful, but instead she simmered with anger. The most terrifying thing about the entire experience was the fact that Alice had no remorse at all. "He deserved it." was all she would say. Jake knew Edward had not deserved the brutal attack; but she still had Jake where she wanted him, submissive to her. And, with no child to contend with, Alice felt a sense of freedom. She finally had Jake back to herself. And so, their life went on without Edward.

Real estate went well for Jake and kept him busy

with managing all the sales and houses being built. He loved to look out at the beautiful lake, the tall fir trees, the magnificent peaks of the Olympia Mountain Range and of course, Mt Rainier. Eventually, after a few years, Jake tired of his real estate job and when he was offered a job at Boeing, the aircraft manufacturing corporation, he took it. He was ready for a change of scenery; to get away from the memory of the last days with his son. Alice was ready for a change too. She was used to moving, resettling, making new "friends". She had tired of the women in the area of Bellevue. Or perhaps they tired of her. It was difficult for Alice to be "nice" to those women. Her real self would show through; demeaning and rude comments do not usually settle very well in the friendship arena. But, home life was better. Once again the couple would go to the military shooting range and practice target shooting; a sport both excelled in. They dined in restaurants on the Seattle pier, walked in the woods near their home and entertained guests where Alice was a kind hostess. Alice was comfortable hosting dinner parties with another couple; she controlled the cooking, place settings, conversation. Everything converted back to before custody of Edward and they became somewhat content.

With a move to Redmond, Washington Jake began his position in Everett, Washington with Boeing. He began the position while attending Pacific Lutheran University to complete the Boeing Management Development Program in the commercial airplane division and the certification of Purchasing for the Airframe Industry. It was 1968. As the development of the first "jumbo jet", the Boeing 747, was being completed, Jake was responsible for the plant services facility, he kept equipment operational avoiding machine downtime, assessed work priorities, and attended and frequently facilitated team meetings which took him out of town. He was also responsible for purchasing airframe parts which took him throughout the United States. His skills once again landed him this high interest, high expectations, and highly important position. Those skills included the ability to manage a project's development from inception to completion, effective communication among team members, development and delivery of progress reports, analyses and assessments of development plans and, when needed, recommend change. Nothing new for Jake. And he did his job once again with diligence, integrity, confidentiality.

Alice seemed to like Jake's schedule and did not seem to mind the time he spent away from home. Two home events occurred during that time. The first was the adoption of a Rottweiler who was named Space. Space was a good name Jake and Alice decided because of the space race competition between the United States and the USSR during that time of the Cold War. Jake regularly being out of town on business, decided to let Alice train the dog. Why would she not? She had trained him. The only thing he worried about was if the dog would attack him. He could never be sure her purpose of training anything. He felt a little sorry for the dog, but Alice was actually kinder to the dog than she ever was towards Edward. The second event was the letters that arrived from Edward. He had kept them abreast of his going to El Camino Community College, graduating from University of California-Northridge all in three short years with three majors: Biology, Political Science, and Journalism. He earned his Master's degree in Business from University of California Los Angeles and had begun his career; first Liberty Mutual as an appraiser, then with Texaco as a very young manager. Then, right after the birth of his first child, Edward Lee Jacobs, Jr., Jake's son introduced the new product, Tylenol, to doctors throughout the Los Angeles area for Johnson and Johnson. He was married at age 19 to Mary. Edward often wondered why his father did not respond to any of these letters. Could the reason have been, it was because Alice threw them away before Jake even knew the letters existed or was told anything about them? Jake figured Edward hated him. Jake could not and would not contact Edward. His son would contact him on his own time. And besides, Jake was humiliated and knew he let his son down. You can imagine Jake's surprise and Alice's dismay when Edward called to ask for a visit to their home with his new family. Jake immediately, and with gratefulness to God, agreed to their visit to their home in Redmond. It was January 1, 1970, and Baby Lee was only two months old with screaming colic, and Mary a shy, anxious 22 year old. Why wouldn't she be? Ed had told her all about his childhood. Nevertheless, when they arrived, Jake shook his son's hand and peered at blue-eyed baby Lee with eyes full of love and pride. Instead of the week they had planned, they stayed only three days. It was a tossup on why; Alice's icy silence and forced kindness or the colic causing Lee to scream in pain though out the night at a home that was none too friendly anyway. The good news for father and son was the visit seemed to open up some communication between them. Both were satisfied with that. It was a start.

Alice was becoming restless again. She didn't really like Redmond. It was hard to determine why, but she had a bee in her bonnet to move to Ocean Shores, Washington, right on the beach of the Pacific Ocean. "Why not?" figured Jake. They checked it out and the life style was perfect for them. Ocean views, a golf club to join for socialization, and an apartment for Jake to escape in Everett, Washington so he could do his job. During the week, Jake would drive his Chrysler made vehicle, 162.5 miles to his apartment and back again to Ocean Shores during the weekend. It helped him to cope with his marriage. In fact, things began to go better and better and Jake was feeling that Alice wanted and needed him. What man doesn't love that feeling?

After settling into their new Ocean Shores home they took a short weekend vacation to California. Edward was living in Brea, Orange County, California with his family which included during the 1972 visit, 6 month old Christy. Jake wanted to see them all. So, Edward took a day off from his pharmaceutical position to help Mary host a dinner at home for his father and the wicked step mother. The visit went well with Alice holding her tongue and Jake, being Jake, appreciative and content to be with his son, his daughter in law and his two grandchildren. Probably, it was a good thing they stayed only a few hours, for after all, how long could a person like Alice hold her tongue? The visit meant a great deal to Edward.

Life continued for the Jacobs' with rumors that a job change in Boeing for Jake was forthcoming. It was. But before it did, the Edward Jacobs' family showed up in Ocean Shores for a short visit. It was 1974 and Edward was on his way to his Sammamish High School reunion. Why not stop and say hello to the folks, see their new Ocean Shores home, and bless them with a visit from their grandchildren including 6 month old, Kevin. Did not work out as well as Edward had hoped. Although Jake, Edward, Lee and Christy enjoyed a 9-hole golf game on that fresh Pacific Northwest June day, Mary and Kevin, did not. They stayed home with Alice whose tongue she could not hold this time. She just could not help herself. Invasion into her territory with three kids? Really? Well, poor Mary had to bear Alice's insults about her mothering skills and went so low as to make a comment about her extra weight put on by the last baby. Rude. By the time the happy golfers arrived home, Alice drilled Jake questioning how 9 holes could take so long. Mary could only cry. Edward thanked his father for the wonderful day on the course, piled his family into his car, and drove back to California to stabilize everyone's emotions; even his own! He missed his 10 year reunion.

Edwards Air Force base was home of a military project involving Boeing. Just because the Cold War was not a hot one, it didn't mean it would not become one and the United States military needed to be prepared. That meant new military defense missiles, rockets, and jets. A Boeing military project during 1974 was the reason Jake accepted a position that required a close-lipped manager. His position was located on the base collaborating with the military and Boeing team on production and management of their secret project. Having once again obtained a military security clearance he pursued his job with enthusiasm and diligence. Having sold their Ocean Shores house, Alice and Jake settled into their newly built home in Hemet, California. Once again, as Jake worked, Alice took care of their home life. And once again his job called him out of town during the week with Jake living on the air force base and a commute home during the weekends.

With suspicions of communism and espionage out of control during the Cold War Era, building defense weapons could be a dangerous job as Jake one day found out while touring the Boeing defense weapons manufacturing plant. As he and two Army officers, including a General, were inspecting some Boeing manufactured parts one early morning, Jake heard a thundering crash not a foot behind him. Jake had nerves of steel. He, after all, had been a dive bomber in the Pacific during the war and experienced far greater unnerving sounds than he heard behind him, but this one made the officers and him jump! As they turned around, they saw a huge piece of metal, a missile part, behind them. A near miss. Just two steps saved them from being smashed and killed. Immediately, they looked above to see where this massive weapon of possible death had come. The only way it could have fallen was if someone planned it. They saw no one! Jake had the jitters about walking that plant from then on. He knew someone was telling the military, and him, something. Those were strange and uneasy times for America. During air raid drills children were trained to crawl beneath their school desks, as though that would stop a nuclear bomb from killing them. Bomb shelters were built onto homes like swim pools would be built in more secure times. Everyone was on alert!

In the summer of 1980, Edward and his three children arrived for a purpose to the Hemet home of his parents. Mary, Edward's wife, had separated leaving Edward with his three young children. Edward's world had been blown apart. He deeply loved his wife and he had thought they had a good marriage. Desperate, he needed someone to take his three children for a week while he traveled internationally for his pharmaceutical job. Alice and Jake had agreed they would babysit the 8, 6 and 4 year olds. Relieved and with great thankfulness, Edward bid farewell and off he went to do what he needed to do to support his children. Jake knew it would be a long week. Alice knew she would survive, even if the others did not. She took control. Since she was not as good with kids as she was with dogs, the youngsters did not train well. Jake was the calm, quiet force during the week. The children loved him, but he could do little to stop Alice's babysitting style which did not go well with his three beautiful grandchildren.

Finally, Edward made it back on time, the children survived and gleefully ran into his arms, and off they went back to their home in Pleasanton, California; safe again. Before Edward and his young children left Hemet, both Jake and Alice tried to convince him to have a house built in Hemet so he could be closer to them. Edward could not believe his ears. Really? They think that would be good for everyone? When Edward mentioned it to the kids, they began to cry; all three of them. "Please, don't do that to us Daddy." they begged. Alice was awful. She was mean. He had to agree and the move for the four of them did not happen. And as they drove off, Jake worried for his son. He knew what it was like to be abandoned. Now Edward, too, had been abandoned by his mother and a woman he loved. He hoped his son would not grab someone else on the rebound as he had done! He prayed he would find his true love and find happiness. That is what he wanted for Edward, and had wanted for himself!

The Seven Hills Golf Club drew Jake's attention as it needed a director. A director Jake was. Since he had retired from Boeing on February 1, 1982, Jake needed something other than reading to challenge his brain and focus his energies. Managing a golf course was it. Alice and Jake had been members of the Seven Hills Golf Club ever since they moved into their Hemet home. It catered to mostly seniors, and the Café on the Greens was superb, relaxing and social. Many a morning and afternoon the Jacobs' would meet friends there and enjoy a relaxing meal. Jake no longer had his escape to an apartment, so he acclimated to his environment as he had always done. He kept his words few, remained calm and soft spoken and let Alice be the commanding officer. It just worked better that way. He took orders well and only now and then did he disagree; always with kindness and logic. Life was quite good until colon cancer struck.

Chapter 22 -- Changes

Jake sank deeper down under the sheets of the Edwards Air Force Base Military Hospital bed. As he laid there thinking, he was struck by all the near misses in his life; Marine in China during the 1930's, the training plane crash, dive bombing over the Pacific. Not one injury and he was not about to die from cancer. It actually angered him that he was lying in a bed waiting his fate and not a damn thing he could do about it! As he simmered with anger, Alice called Edward. He was remarried to Linda and they had just moved to Seattle, all eight of them. Edward had three stepchildren. Although busy with his new pharmaceutical job as Vice President in cancer drug development at Adria, Edward did not hesitate to grab the first flight he could get and was at his father's side faster than Alice thought possible. Edward was surprised, no, he was shocked, to see the fear in her eyes. Huh? Perhaps she really did love his father. Since Edward was in the medical cancer field, he fully understood the consultation between the doctor and the two of them. As they stressed together in the waiting room during his father's colon cancer surgery, not a harsh or unkind word was spoken between Alice and himself. As the doctor came out, it was a tossup on who jumped up first. Both son and wife had a lot to lose. But lose they did not. The doctor had cut out the tumor and the prognosis was the cancer was gone. He would be fine. A near miss again.

While recovering, Alice waited on Jake hand and foot. There were times she even let him have two scoops of ice cream. That Thanksgiving Edward flew into Hemet after a week's business overseas. He packed his father and wife into his Dad's Dodge Chrysler and drove to Seattle to spend the holiday with Edward's huge family and new home on a very prestigious golf course. Jake was thrilled to meet his three step grandchildren and their mother. She was kind, a good cook, and willing to make everyone comfortable, including Alice who was well behaved on the trip. He had quiet talks with Edward telling him how proud he was of his accomplishments and asked many questions about his job and what it entailed. Jake, a food lover, wolfed down his dinner, but not the turkey. He hated turkey. But, Linda knew that before he arrived and had a ham also. What a gal Edward had picked this time, even though he had the feeling Edward may have been on the rebound. He would not have blamed him for that. He needed a wife; someone to care for his children and to be with him. Like Jake, Edward did not like to be alone. When Jake found out Linda was Edward's first wife's cousin, he snickered which was his way of roaring with laughter. He shared with them that his step mother was actually his biological mother's cousin. Something else he and his son had in common. Lee, Kevin, and Christy were teens by then and Jake, for the first time in his life, realized how fast time was passing by. With everyone pleased with the Thanksgiving Seattle visit, Alice drove her husband home to Hemet.

They knew he needed to take time off managing projects so Jake and Alice decided to sell their home in Hemet and buy a motor home. So as proud owners of a Winnebago they stored all their belongings at a local storage facility and off they and Space #2 went to roam the great country Jake helped to save. The motor home was cozy. It consisted of the usual; a double bed, little kitchen, a pull out table, small bathroom with a tiny shower, and two massive comfortable chairs in the front for driver and the person riding shotgun. Jake had traveled cross country several times before and in many different ways, but never in a big 'ole bus like that! He loved it. The power of choosing which highways to travel on, which diners to eat at, campsites to sleep in, and sites to see! It was fantastic, for a while. Within six months they had tired of it. Besides the small freezer could only hold what Alice called, "real food"; no ice cream. As they roamed through Phoenix they considered retiring there, too hot! Santé Fe was gorgeous; maybe. San Diego was beautiful; too expensive. Las Cruces; perfect! As a retired military town, it also boasted New Mexico State University. With the Organ Mountains towering to the east, the population of less than 100,000, only an hour and a half from Ft. Bliss in El Paso, Texas, 20 minutes away from the White Sands Missile Base and average temperatures way less than Phoenix, Alice and Jake had found their retirement home! Nothing like being around military people! That had been their life together from the beginning. They understood military. So as they purchased a three bedroom home, Jake attended the weekly gathering at the Veteran's administration. He was anxious to meet the people in Las Cruces and begin his social life. His first coffee at the weekly veterans meeting, he met what would become the best friend of his life, Eldon, a retired Air Force veteran. Eldon and his wife had lived in Las Cruces for two years, native born Nebraskan, he had a big smile, a big sense of humor, and a bigger heart. He, like Jake, was fiercely loyal to his mate and an American patriot through and through. He, also like Jake, was a thinker and an analyzer. The difference was that Eldon was a talker; he liked to throw out a thought and have everyone express their opinion about it. Eldon engaged his new friend in all kinds of talk. Since Jake never shared his battle stories with anyone, he did love to share the fun ones such as the private on the roof! Eldon shared a lot of his fun ones but Jake especially liked the story about Eldon being in charge of security at the military personnel bar in London. He was used to different groups of bands entertaining the troops in the bar on Friday nights, but one group he remembered quite vividly. The four member male band, all in their early 20's, long hair, and were in his eyes, just a group of low life hoods. Imagine his surprise when only two years later he watched "the hoodlums" perform on the Ed Sullivan show. Yup. The Beatles. Jake got a chuckle out of that one! Another commonality between the two friends was they both had demanding spouses, spurring the buddies to spend more time away from home; but not to the point of neglect. They also liked and needed to have a purpose in life.

As his Dad was settling in Las Cruces, Edward had been living in Pleasanton, California and working as a CFO for Super Gen, a cancer drug development company. He also had a home in Phoenix, Arizona where he had recovered after a heart attack in 1991 while running in the Atlantic Airport to catch a business flight. Thank God, Linda was traveling with him, called 911 and he received immediate treatment. When Jake heard about this event, he became more scared than he had ever been in his life. Jake prayed for his son. He also vowed he would try to become closer to him, but that was hard for Jake. He called him more often and made a visit to Phoenix to see him. His way of talking to his son was usually asking questions about his job and then a reply, "Sounds like a good job." Jake would always be Jake and Edward just had to realize that was Jake's way of complimenting him. Would they every get close? That was the question they both asked themselves.

Back in Las Cruces, one day Eldon threw out the idea of perhaps they should do something to honor all the veterans who lived in Las Cruces. Putting their two logical and brilliant heads together, Jake and Eldon came up with a Veteran's Day Parade. Why not? Had there ever been one in Las Cruces before? Why hadn't there been? The city was stuffed full of military retirees, and college kids. Why not honor the men who were and are responsible for protecting America? This was no small feat! City permits had to be issued, funds had to be found, enthusiasm from the population had to be stirred, girl and boy scout troops had to be prepared, bands had to be played, streets had to be closed, and the most important in the planners' minds was, the veterans had to be honored. Jake felt he, in a small way, was paying back all the service men and women who were injured or killed in the wars. They deserved respect. Eldon and Jake organized, managed and succeeded in making the first Veteran's Day Parade happen in Las Cruces. What a success! Every year after 1992, there has been the parade with announcements printed, broadcasted, and delivered; thanks to Jake and Eldon.

Jake was not one to just sit around for long. Sure, he enjoyed watching his Arkansas Razorback football games. He had never had the time to just sit and watch them; in fact, he had forgotten about them. Jake's only team he treasured was his Razorbacks; certainly not the LSU Tigers! He could not get into the Dodgers or the Mariners. While living in Bellevue he did get wrapped up in the Seahawks, the Seattle football NFL team. He would watch them, but he wouldn't go out of his way. The Razorbacks he would, but Alice didn't like to watch football so the games were far and few between. Since sitting wasn't entirely working for him, other than hanging out with Eldon, he did not have much to do. Oh sure, Alice and he would have couples over to play Canasta or another card game, go to dinner with friends, have them come to the house sometimes, but the inactivity, especially for his brain, was making Jake antsy! He decided to become a member appointed by the city council of the Rent Review Commission. Acting like mediators of disputes between mobile home tenants and park owners, Jake was in his zone. He was used to managing people, analyzing places, and forming solutions. It also was just one more way of being out of the house now and then.

Alice liked their new home and city except the house they bought was right by the freeway. Why did Jake agree to buy it? Just because she was the one who wanted it, he should have told her "no." Fat chance of that! Although she once again settled into a house, she constantly complained of the street noise and the neighbors next door. What was Jake to do? Buy a new house. Edward had not seen his father for quite some time, but when he learned he would be moving and was told of the neighborhood and price of the house, he decided to go to Las Cruces. His father and him struck a deal that if Edward put in an extra $10,000, the payment would be less and more manageable for his dad's income. Upon selling the house, Edward would get his money back. Okay with Edward. In fact, he decided to buy the one next door for his Dad to use as a rental. Edward's reasoning was twofold; his Dad needed more to do and he could manage the rental and he could pick his own neighbors; a good thing considering Alice's moodiness about others. It was done! Father and son felt their relationship was coming together a little more. Being the men they were, neither told the other how he felt. So, it went on...

New Mexico State University was the destination of Jake's youngest grandson, Kevin, as he began his college years in 1995. Delighted that Kevin was in Las Cruces,

Edward felt his going to the university in Las Cruces would give him and his grandfather some quality time. Edward was wrong! Since his step sister, Suzie, was a sophomore there, Kevin drug her with him to see his grandfather and the much dreaded step grandmother, who did not like the word mother much less grandmother. It did not go well! Alice ridiculed, demeaned, and was not a good hostess. They never went back. So much for his relationship, Grandpa. However, Jake was sickened by it and he had a telescope he used to watch the campus during the day and caught site of the young handsome man who looked very similar to himself in his youth. That was all Jake could do and that had to be enough. Although he saw his son and Linda more often because of their coming to see their children, he did not see Kevin until he and Alice attended Mandy and Kevin's wedding in December 1999. After missing so many events in his son's and now his grandsons' lives, he did make that one! It was beautiful and Jake was honored to have attended. Alice held her tongue, thank God.

On February 15, 2001 Edward and Linda threw Mr. and Mrs. Nelson Edward Jacobs a 50 year wedding anniversary party at the Hilton Hotel in Las Cruces. The number of guests were well above the amount Edward had expected. And he was thrilled. His father had become a very intricate part of the community, winning the hearts and loyalty of everyone he met. Alice was well known too and somewhat accepted. People seemed to be coming out of the woodwork and Jake greeted each one. The ball room was decorated to the nines with fresh roses, balloons, white tablecloths, napkins printed with Alice and Jake on them, a local band that knew the 40 and 50's tunes, a dance floor and a huge cake. It was perfect. Eldon who had never met Edward knew Jake's son must love the couple very much to put on such a huge celebration.

Jake took great pride in being a citizen of Las Cruces for many reasons. One of the reasons was the Baatan Memorial Death March held every March to honor those U. S. Marines forced to march a very long distance by the Japanese during World War II, later known as the Baatan Death March. The parallel to his own experiences was touching to Jake, for he had a near miss when he was not part of the 4th China Marines to disembark off the military transport ship at the Philippines back in 1941. A very large percentage of those Marines who were brutally killed, beaten, and starved were from New Mexico; thus, the commemoration in Las Cruces each year. Thousands of people show up to walk in the 26.2 trek beginning at the White Sands Missile Range. Very emotional. Very special.

In June of 2001, Edward was working out of Boston, Massachusetts when his father called him about Alice. She had suffered a heart attack and needed surgery. Edward immediately boarded the next available flight to El Paso, rented a car and drove like a bat out of hell to be with his father during that time. Jake, rightfully so, was upset. His wife of 50 years was direly ill. Edward stayed with him during the surgeries and made sure his father's needs were met. They went to eat at Jake's favorite restaurants, watched a couple baseball games on TV even though Jake didn't really like baseball, and talked a little. It was obvious Jake was a little shaken. Upon getting Alice home again, setting up nurses to come in, and home cleaning and cooking help for them, Edward went home. Edward called his father more often to check on the happenings in his life and sent him pictures of his five year old great grandson, Christopher who was Kevin's child. When he received a call from Alice that his father needed a pacemaker later that year, he once again boarded a plane, rented a car, and was there before and after the procedure to be with his father. He loved his father, very much.

Alice was in and out of the hospital with her heart problems. She did not get any nicer but then, she really did not get any meaner either. On Thanksgiving of 2002, Edward had joined his father and his stepmother for Thanksgiving. Alone? Strange. Where was Linda? Why was Edward with them for Thanksgiving? He surely was not there to cook, he did not do that! Upon arrival, Edward explained to his father in private that Linda and he had separated. The kids, all six of them, were grown and gone. They had grown away from each other; another sad ending of a marriage for Edward. Jake talked quietly to him. He told him he understood and a man had to do what a man had to do, "Just take care of her. Do the right thing." was his father's advice. Of course, he would, for Edward had the integrity of his father. Eldon and his wife hosted Thanksgiving. Edward ate turkey, but his dad did not.

On July 3, 2004 Lee, Jake's oldest grandson, landed his private one engine plane at the Las Cruces airstrip, helped his father grab his bags and called his grandfather from his cell phone. Alice was very sick. She was in hospice care in the house with only a few days expected to live. As Jake and Lee talked in the living room, Edward said good bye to Alice. He told her it was okay to die and that he would take care of Jake for her. She took Edward's hand and said, "I'm sorry Edward." And he replied, "I forgive you." What a way to go! As Jake hugged both his relations goodbye to fly back to Phoenix, he went into his wife's room and sat next to her bed. He held her hands in his and waited. He did love her. She was a tough one, but she took care of him and they had some good times. He kissed her forehead. She grinned. And then God took her away. He patted Space #3 on the head and said a prayer. He did not cry. Lee and Edward came back on July 5th to help Jake spread ashes of Alice in the spot up in the Organ Mountains she had requested. They all noticed with a grin that the ashes were still a bit hot, fresh from the oven. As they said goodbye, Edward and Jake knew Alice actually had some good qualities and Edward had learned a lot from her about himself and life. The rest of her ashes were buried. Rest in peace in Ft. Bliss National Cemetery as you wait for your husband of 53 years.

Chapter 23 -- Oh No! Not again...

Jake's sister, Elizabeth, lived in Houston and upon hearing the news of her brother's wife dying, convinced him to get on a plane and visit her at her Texas home. He was excited about the prospect but he had to wait until Edward's visit to Las Cruces. It had only been six weeks since Alice left him, but he was lonely. Jake and his son dined at I-Hop and Applebees, watched a movie and Edward found out some new information from his father. His father asked him lots of questions about work, as he always did and when asked by Edward how he was doing without Alice, his father had replied, "It's kind of lonely around here. I am going to Houston to see my sister." They both agreed that would be a good idea, but Edward was skeptical because his father had never been close to his sister before. Why now? And then again, why not now? One thing Edward knew, it was nice not to hear Alice screeching across the house, "JAKE!"

Eldon agreed to take Jake to and from the airport. He was always available if someone needed him, especially his best friend, Jake. And besides, Eldon was afraid of Jake's driving. He would always tell him, "You were a great pilot, but are a lousy driver." Jake's response was his little smirk and a chuckle. Good thing he had continued buying Chrysler products. Since the death of Alice, the two of them became closer; more coffees together, planning the Veteran's Day parade, long walks. He felt that Jake was lonely; he didn't know what he had up his sleeve though. No one ever knew what Jake was planning or thinking; he was not one to share a lot of information.

Jake was gone a week and upon arriving home announced to Eldon and his wife and to Edward that he had a girlfriend. What? That was fast! His sister in Houston had plans for Jake; to reunite with a woman he had met before many, many years ago, Betty! Betty was a mere two years younger than Jake at the ripe old age of 83. She had a southern, Texan drawl, her husband had died nine years previous, had two daughters and a son, with several grandchildren in the Houston area. She had lived in the same house for over 40 years. With blue eyes, she had a sweet disposition always thanking people and smiling. Jake was quite taken with her. In September of 2004, Jake drove his new love to Scottsdale, Arizona to meet his son and his son's fiancée, Kerry. A trip to the Grand Canyon was the plan since Betty had never seen it. When the couple arrived, after directing Jake and his love to the two guest rooms, Edward decided to let them decide if they would stay in the same room or not. They both slept in the same room which had only one queen size bed in it. Okay. "Whatever works for them," thought the host and hostess. The next day's Grand Canyon trip was enjoyable for all four of the travelers. Edward drove his car, they stopped in Williams, Arizona for lunch at a quaint, western café, walked to the edge of the canyon, took pictures, and safely arrived home late at night with everyone happy. Betty just went on and on about how beautiful the Grand Canyon was. What a sweetheart! Dad and his love drove back to New Mexico the next day. Not a week passed by and Edward answered the phone. It was his father with big news. He was getting married! At the ages 83 and 85. Why waste time?

On January 20, 2005 in Houston, Texas another Mrs. Nelson Edward Jacobs arrived. It was a great weekend for Jake with his son, his son's fiancé, and his two grandchildren Christy and Lee attending the Friday family dinner and the Saturday church wedding. Friday's dinner was hosted by Edward at the favorite steakhouse of the bride and groom. It fed a large number of Betty's family including her two daughters and her son along with their spouses and most of their children. There were toasts and laughter. Everyone was happy. As all the grandchildren of the happy couple went to a nearby bar to continue the celebration, the rest went to their respectful places and went to sleep in preparation for the wedding the next day. Edward was thrilled to hear Betty saying so sweetly, "Nelson" to his father. Life was good and his dad deserved to have a kind, sweet wife. On Saturday afternoon in the local Houston Baptist Church Betty approached her groom to "Here Comes the Bride" and looked as radiant as an 83 year old woman could be with flowers in her hair and matching flowers on her walker. A reception followed with music from the 1930's and 1940's, a beautiful pink and white cake, and everyone in the room gushing over this happy couple. There were more family than friends, but no one really noticed or questioned that, until much later. Jake invited everyone over to Betty's house where she played the piano and remained the center of attention. As agreed, Jake stayed in Houston for six weeks. The plan was they would switch homes to live in every couple of months. They were set!

Jake enjoyed having someone in the house again and he liked to be active. Good thing, because he walked to the mailbox every day, made the meals under Betty's watchful eye so that he did it her way, cleaned the kitchen, and basically kissed her ass. She was a southern girl and she liked to be waited on. Jake really did not mind. Good thing he and Alice had employed a weekly cleaning lady, Carmel. She did a terrific job, and Jake did not have to worry about that! Betty's daughters would come and go. One had an artistic streak and began selling her western art at the local fairs in Las Cruces. Jake enjoyed both her daughters, Barbara and Susan. Each were ecstatic that Jake had married their mother and seemed very supportive of him for they knew at times their mother could be "a little demanding", but like they told Jake, "You married her, so good luck!" Jake would always laugh at that but he wasn't worried. He and Betty attended Edward and Kerry's wedding on December 22, 2005 in Scottsdale. Love was all around!

In 2006 after one of Jake's well checks with his doctor, he found out he needed a new pacemaker. Of course, he had regular phone calls from his son Edward, so Edward was aware of his health. He made plans to be at the hospital when his dad got the device put in. Kerry was there also. The time his Dad was going into the procedure was 9:00 am, so

Kerry and Edward were at the hospital by 8:00 am to ensure their pre surgery visit with dad. Jake kept asking for Betty. His son said she was on her way, which she was. Problem was that Barbara and Betty did not arrive until 30 minutes after he was out of surgery. Where were they? Getting ready. Their excuse? "We thought the surgery would take longer." Weak.

Everyone makes mistakes so Betty's lateness was forgiven by all. Back and forth from Las Cruces to Houston they traveled, but by 2007 Jake decided the drive was too much for him so either Barbara or Susan would fly out to drive them back. They would always come by air and who picked them up from El Paso International Airport? Eldon of course! Eldon loved helping people and he found Barbara and Susan to be quite talkative and friendly. They would even tell about their mother and how difficult she could be. Never did they offer to pay for the gas or pay for the lunch that Eldon many times bought for them. He didn't mind. He was and still is a giver!

Edward and Kerry would fly in from Phoenix every other month for a weekend. Both were still working, Edward as a CEO/ CFO and Kerry as a teacher. The first order of business was Betty's favorite place to eat dinner on Friday evenings. It started out as the Cracker Barrel, but a waitress made a mistake by sitting Betty in a place she did not like, so no more Cracker Barrel. Then it was Applebees, but someone gave her cold coffee. Big mistake. No more Applebees. And so it went. Jake never seemed too annoyed about it. It was what it was and there were lots of places in Las Cruces to eat.

Jake was surprised on April 4, 2008, his 90th Birthday. Edward had planned a surprise party for him at his favorite restaurant, Cattle Baron. Betty's daughters were there, her nephew and his wife were there, neighbors were there, Eldon was there, and Kevin, his grandson, with his family was there. Christopher, Becca and Bella were ages 12, 5 and 1. Jake was the center of attention and it was a delightful time for all, especially Jake. Edward and Kerry stayed at the local Towns Place Suites by Marriott so Betty's daughters could stay in the house. The next morning, they swung by to say goodbye and kiss dad goodbye. It was all good, until the next visit.

Jake had been noticing how Betty seemed more and more angry. Granted she had her sweet moments when she wanted something. But, ever since they were married, she became more and more demanding and less and less appreciative. Her complaining was constant. Although he took her to her exercise lessons at the swim pool, cooked meals, cleaned, waited on her, got her what she wanted, watched only her shows, listened to her music, she complained. When other people were around, Betty was her usual sweet self with every thank you dripping in honey. Jake was patient. Dutiful. Loyal. That was Jake! Upon the advice of all their children, they got themselves "the button" to push in case there was an emergency. Everyone felt better until it was ascertained that the alert buttons were kept in a bowl in the middle of the dinner table. What good was that? When

Kerry encouraged Betty to wear one, she bit Kerry's head off. Where did that nasty comment come from? When Edward mentioned the eggs were three months out of date, he lost his head too. Nasty! Kerry and Edward learned to throw bad food out when no one was looking. Jake saw them do it, he grinned his grin and thanked them for doing it discreetly; after all, he did not want to get a nasty comment! When they visited, Kerry would always ask what they would like her to cook for dinner. Jake always had ideas so she followed them, but Betty didn't like this or that! Kerry decided to bake her one of her favorite Marie Calendar Chicken Pot pies one evening, while cooking Jake a different meal. Betty had a fit! She scolded Kerry on how each person should eat the same thing; after all, that is how she raised her kids. Kerry explained it was no problem and that she wanted everyone to enjoy their dinner. Betty did not speak to Kerry the rest of the evening and it did not go well later that evening when instead of Lawrence Welk, Betty's favorite show, an Irish music show was on. She insisted Edward lied to her and scanned the TV guide for an hour to prove it. She couldn't because he had not lied. Nasty little woman. Edward was beginning to worry what his father had gotten himself into, but decided to stay out of it. His dad seemed content enough. But, what did the future hold?

Always on their best behavior and swearing to one another in their rental car from El Paso to Las Cruces that they would appease Betty the entire weekend for Dad, Edward and Kerry tried to keep their patience and sense of humor. It was very hard. Betty would start out liking her pepperoni pizza from Dion's, but it would go downhill from there. She loved going to the commissary to grocery shop. She hated Albertsons because she once got a too ripe banana there and swore she would never go back. Jake tried to convince her and told her the story of his friend, Joe. She could care less. No more Albertsons for anyone in that household. The commissary took at least 2 ½ hours once inside. The store was smaller than any Albertsons, but Betty had to look at everything and move slowly, very slowly. Edward pushed the cart, Jake walked next to Betty, and Kerry jumped to service when Betty would bark, "How much is this?" and Edward would put the number of items she told him to into the cart. Jake grinned probably because he knew how much Betty loved going to the commissary. He was actually amused by her antics. The other two people in the party were not. Eventually, Edward would stay in Jake's Chrysler van and wait before he lost his temper with his annoying step mother. After Jake paid the bill and they were back at home, Betty always asked how many bags there were. What? She didn't want to be ripped off. She was always worried Kerry would take something out of the bags and make it her own. Kerry didn't. That evening on the way to dinner for Jake's 91st birthday, Betty complained to Kerry as they sat in the back seat. "This town doesn't have any good restaurants. Jake slams the cabinets all the time. I hate that." Complain, complain, complain. Kerry tried to sooth her and reminded her it was Jake's birthday. "Let's make it happy for him." At the restaurant Jake ordered for his rude wife, went to the salad bar for her, got the waiter to get her new coffee three times. Kerry and Edward were quiet and tried to carry on a cheerful, birthday type conversation. Good grief!

Summer of 2009 came around and Jake was feeling poorly. He could not figure out exactly what was wrong, but he was out of sorts. He continued his life with Betty; their home life, hosting her daughters visits that lasted weeks at a time, having dinners with Eldon and his wife (who Betty did not like and Jake knew Eldon's wife did not like her!), and Eldon continued to be at the daughters' beckon call to and from the airport. Finally, Jake had to go to the hospital for tests which showed his colon cancer had returned. Immediately, Edward and Kerry were in Las Cruces. Edward, once again, consulted with doctors on what they could and would do for his father. Betty was comforted by her daughters who arrived almost as quickly as Edward. Betty sat and fretted and moaned and groaned. She was in all the meetings of the doctors and Edward. She worried about herself; what would she do with Jake in the hospital? Everyone worried about her when, seriously, they should have been more worried about Jake. Edward was. The final decision was a colonoscopy. Without it, he would have died.

For years Jake had been waking up at two in the morning, getting out of bed, hitting the button on the coffee pot, grabbing a cookie, and sitting in his recliner in the living area. He was as quiet as a mouse and this was his time. He sipped his coffee, ate his cookie, and contemplated life. Sometimes he would take a few minutes to write in his journal about his military life. Sometimes he just sat and thought. He always fell asleep and woke up in time to help Betty out of bed, get her pills for her, bring her a cup of coffee and make her breakfast. Kerry began making him oatmeal cookies which became his favorite of all time. Every time Edward and Kerry came over, she brought the cookies and even made different kinds to go along with them so Betty could choose her favorite. Jake liked that Edward and Kerry brought the cookies for him; it made him feel special. One morning while the kids were there Jake was annoyed to hear Betty say, "Nelson always wakes me up when he gets up in the morning. He should stop doing it." Jake knew he did not wake her up. She was asleep. He needed some time to himself and he felt perturbed at her and mostly at himself for feeling annoyed with her.

Jake could no longer serve Betty as he had in the past. After his couple months in rehab at the nearby nursing home, he came home only to feel frustrated. Betty had 24/7 care from the local Home Instead office; a facility that supplies nurses for in home care. Jake felt he was letting his wife down. He had always been able to take care of himself and to do what he wanted physically. He was strong and capable, but after the colonoscopy, he felt useless. Betty's daughters did not help his feelings of inadequacy; they insisted their mother was his wife and he was financially responsible for her! Betty did not help either. She would not look at his opening where tubes protruded out to catch the waste from his body. She was sickened by it. A nurse came every day to change the bag and tried to teach Betty how to do it. Betty refused. She was disgusted. Jake was embarrassed, but he was a survivor and would acclimate to this major change in his life. When his son and Kerry once again showed up, the nurse helped Kerry to learn to change the bag. Not on Kerry's list of things she liked to do, but she did it. Betty, upon greeting Edward and Kerry at the door of her home, grabbed them both and led them to the bathroom screaming, "Look at the mess Nelson made. There is poop everywhere! What am I suppose to do?" The visitors were appalled, not by the mess, but by the inhumane way Betty handled the situation. Kerry quietly cleaned it up. Shame on Betty. Jake was the victim here, not her! But it got worse. Nurses sent from Home Instead quit; some within a week, others within a month. Jake tried soothing them, they liked Jake. He was kind, soft spoken, but when the woman of the house humiliated them and chastised them, they quit. Home Instead director called Edward several times in hopes he could talk to his dad and help tame the beast, Betty. He tried, but to no avail. As long as Jake could serve Betty and give her everything she wanted, the marriage was fine. After Jake's surgery, it suffered, but not as much as Jake. Not only was he feeling unmanly, he was physically abused. He began getting out of bed in the middle of the night earlier, just to avoid the hitting of Betty's fists. He had sores on his head that came from being worried and heart sickened. When Betty's daughters showed up, they called Arizona to report how hard Jake was on their mother. What? Well, their mom would yell at him, hit him, but he did not always sooth her. For example, because of his cancer and surgery, they were no longer able to travel back and forth to Houston. Betty wanted to go to Houston and continually told Jake. He would quietly say, "You have your money and I have mine. If you want to go to Houston you can go." That made her daughters mad. Why should their mother use her money when Jake married her? He was responsible for their mother. Don't send her to Houston, then they would have to take care of her and as her oldest daughter, Susan, said, "My mother living in Houston would be a nightmare for me." Wow! The daughters were perfectly clear about who was responsible physically and monetarily for their mother, her husband!

Worried about his father, Edward began going more often to Las Cruces with his wife. Every other week, he was there but he no longer could stay at the house "just in case the girls show up from Houston." That did not set well with Edward. That was his father's house. But he and Kerry decided they would go to the hotel and it would probably be better in the long run. The next visit, Kerry called Jake's house as they traveled in their Hertz rental from the El Paso airport to Las Cruces. No answer; busy. Tried again; same thing. Again; busy. Five times she called to find out what kind of pizza they wanted from Dion. She knew it would have to be the right kind or Betty would have a fit! Busy each time. When they arrived the garage door was open. They entered through the garage, knocked on the door to the house, entered and was blocked by Betty and her walker. They could not get past her. She had fire in her eyes. She was hungry. Why didn't they call? She was expecting to eat. "You people are rude. You didn't call me when you were on your way. Where's my pizza?" Thank goodness Kerry was between Edward and his very rude stepmother because Edward was losing it. With a quick poke in the ribs from Kerry, Edward held his tongue, but his temper was flaring. Kerry explained she had called five times, but the phone was busy. She got a tongue lashing again by the not very nice older woman who was blocking their entry to the house. Edward said, "That's it. We are leaving." Gently, Jake told Betty to move aside and reminded her she was on the phone with her daughter for quite some time. Edward and Kerry went out, bought the pizza, came home and kept their mouths shut, for Jake's sake. Everyone knows how some older people can get a bit cranky, but Betty was out of control. Had it not been for her daughters' stories to Eldon about how difficult their mother was and Christy and Lee's stories from Betty's grandchildren about growing up with their mean spirited grandmother, Edward and Kerry would have thought it was old age. But it wasn't. Jake had married another mean one, but this time, she was self centered and did not care about his father at all. Edward was heart sick. He swore he would never go to see his father again. But he did, he had to...

Jake catered as much as he could to Betty's needs, but it never seemed like enough. As his health improved and he could get around better, he once again began walking to the mailbox each day to get the mail. He enjoyed the two block walk. Sometimes he would chat with a neighbor and sometimes it was just nice to get out of the house and smell the fresh air. Las Cruces had great weather in Jake's mind. It was dry most of the year; hot during the summer days with cool nights, and a skiff of snow now and then during the winters. On one of his summer mail runs, Jake fell in the street. Unable to get up and walk, he slowly crawled up the incline of the street back to his house. Betty, thinking Jake took way too long to get the mail, went to look for him from the opened garage door! There he was in the hot sun, crawling! Betty, with no sunglasses on and standing with her walker, yelled at him, "Nelson. Crawl into the shade! Why are you in the sun? Don't be stupid, crawl in the shade!" Might have been a time to push the emergency button. Oh yeah, it was in the bowl on the table! Just as Jake was almost to his driveway, a UPS truck driver stopped, picked Jake up, and carried him into the house and into his chair and then got him a glass of water. Betty was glad he saved her husband from the sun, but could not resist letting the UPS driver know who the real victim of the fall was; Betty! She did not have her sunglasses on when she glared at him in the sun and that caused her eyes to be worse than before. Good grief!

Jake continued to hire nurses to come to the house to help him care for Betty. Except for the changing of his colonoscopy bags, Jake could get around okay without help. He had more problems taking care of Betty as she was accustomed to being cared for, so for $35.00 per hour, he hired a caregiver to come in and help out. The caregiver would read to Betty, talk with her, make them both food, and on and on. However, the problem continued; no caregiver could handle the emotional abuse Betty dished out. A caregiver would last anywhere from one week to two months; two months if they had a lot of tenacity. But, never did a caregiver stay. Jake had a nurse, Ray, come in twice a week; he was ex military. He had been Jake's nurse for a couple of years and the two got along famously. Unbeknown to Jake at the time, Ray called Edward one afternoon in a frenzy. He was very upset by what he had witnessed. Betty was hitting Jake with his own cane and yelling at him. Jake could do nothing except to cover his face. Ray stopped the tormenting and called Edward. The nurse just knew that if something wasn't done, Betty would soon hurt Jake very badly and he could not be part of it anymore. That was Ray's last day with Jake for he was afraid Betty would seriously hurt Jake. Although he reported this to his superiors, he felt Jake's son should know about it. Edward and Kerry immediately got in their car and hauled ass over to Las Cruces. As Edward took his father outside to talk some reason into him, Kerry stayed in with Betty. The older woman was as sweet as could be to Kerry. Kerry was so disgusted it was a miracle she did not puke! In the meantime, Edward explained to his father he needed to go with his wife into an assistant living facility where they would both be much safer. Since the Arizona couple had already checked out all the senior homes in the area, Edward mentioned a couple to his father. No. Jake wanted no part of that. He knew he could take care of matters on his own. After all, he always had! Edward and Kerry contacted Betty's daughters, but they did not seem concerned. Of course, it wasn't their mother being beat up. Edward and Kerry left the next day with Jake explaining he was taking Betty to the doctor the next week and hopefully he could give her some new meds. It was a heart sickening ride back to Scottsdale. The only light hearted side was Edward telling Kerry what his father said about his wife or wives; "I sure know how to pick 'em!" Boy, did he!

Thinking that Betty's daughters, "the girls", were on the same page as they were, Edward and Kerry called them often to see what they thought of the New Mexico happenings. Neither gave much information except Jake needed to up the nurse time with their mother because she wanted someone to read to her. The girls spent a lot of time in Las Cruces at Jake's house, drove Jake's van, had Jake pay for groceries and dinners, and continued using Eldon for free rides to and from the airport. Edward and Kerry were reprimanded by both of the girls because they spent lots of time in Las Cruces and the Arizona people only came for a couple days at a time. Of course, the girls were retired; Edward and Kerry were not! So if the girls were spending so much time there, why weren't they looking out for the welfare of the older couple? The care giving hours went up when they were there. Jake paid for it! When the Arizona couple was there, they made sure care givers did not come; they took care of Jake and Betty! It began to not make a lot of sense. Also, even though Betty was always a handful and mean, she was getting worse. Kerry and Edward began going every 7 to 10 days, to insure the safety of Dad. The girls as well as Jake and Betty still refused to even talk about going to an assisted living home. Not good!

Jake thought he heard someone hammering nails into the wall next to the bedroom. No. It was someone knocking at his door at 2 am. What? As he stumbled with his cane, he opened the door to four uniformed police officers. Betty somehow had managed to get herself out of bed and into her walker. She was standing next to Jake. The problem was that the Jacobs' garage had five bullet holes through it and the officers wanted to see the inside and question the residents. Sure enough! Not only were there five bullet holes in the garage door, but the van had been hit by three of them. Lucky one didn't hit the gas tank. Jake considered that a near miss since he had just filled the gas tank that evening. Seemed that shots were heard by neighbors and the police came out! Edward and Kerry upon arriving at the home the next Friday evening, heard of the event! Scary situation! But, thankfully, no one was hurt, but what really happened? Why their garage door? The Arizona Jacobs' had a theory; some home care giver was angry and it was paybacks. No one was ever arrested for the incident, but Betty, in all her self centered wisdom exclaimed over the entire affair, "There those policemen were looking at me when I answered the door and I was in my night gown! They should not have done that! It was rude." Hello? The house just got shot up!

On June 5, 2013 Edward got the dreaded phone call; Jake had been seriously hurt and was in the hospital. The call came from the Home Instead director because their caregiver was at the scene and explained the event. Betty had taken Jake's cane and was trying to hit the caregiver with it. Jake, hearing the yelling, hobbled over to Betty, tried to grab the cane away from her or pull her away. As he did so, she fell on top of him, breaking his hip. Furious, Edward and Kerry jumped into their car and drove to Las Cruces with a phone call to Betty's oldest daughter. She already knew about it because she had been informed by the authorities that her mother was in the psychiatric ward at the state hospital in Las Cruces. Susan was not happy about the situation. Neither was Kerry who had called her. Kerry was very blunt about her mother causing Jake's injury. Susan had responded that when she was there a couple weeks before, Jake had taken the garbage container out to the curb and had fallen. That was when he broke his hip. Really? What a lie! She also explained she nor her sister could possibly go to Las Cruces right then because one had foot surgery and the other had serious heart problems. They, somehow, arrived not 8 hours after the Arizona couple. Quick flights! The girls and the Arizona people never saw each other again.

Jake was taken into surgery the next day, June 6, his son's birthday. The caring physicians put pins in his hip, discussed his injury with Edward, and kept him in the hospital for a week; just long enough for the trip back to Arizona, work, and back again a few days later. Jake was put into the

New Mexico Rehabilitation Center next to the hospital; a new facility with excellent care! To Jake's surprise, on the second day of rehab, his new lawyer showed up with a document to be signed for a new Power of Attorney. Jake was bewildered. Why did he have a new lawyer? He had met his new lawyer the day before and she had asked who he wanted the Power of Attorney to be; he had said his son. She said that was not a good idea; he was already his Power of Attorney and she advised against him. Eldon was Jake's final choice although the lawyer had suggested Susan, Betty's oldest daughter. Why her? That did not make sense to Jake, thank God! The lawyer had conveniently shown up when Edward arrived and went into Jake's room. The lawyer's plan was to have Eldon and Edward in the room at the same time so Jake could tell his son and his best friend about the change. He also told Edward he had changed his will. Okay. Edward as well as Eldon, was confused by all the changes and worried about his father's financial interests and his ability to make major decisions when he was still traumatized from his injury and the way it happened. Why all the changes? Jake assured Edward that he was still in his will and would get something if he died. Edward could not have cared less about that! He just wanted what his father wanted. Who was behind this?

Jake was disappointed with his own physical progress for he was always strong physically and mentally; plus, he wanted to go home. He had found out that Betty was in the hospital and would not be released for several weeks. He was sad. He missed her. Always a southern gentleman and a man of his word, he was committed to his wife. He was responsible for her well being. This feeling was internal but, of course, it didn't help that "the girls" continually visited him and told him every time that he, not anyone else, was responsible for their mother. Medicare and the supplemental insurance ran out on Jake's rehabilitation of his hip, so the doctors decided he needed to go to a nursing facility. Having been to all of them in the town of Las Cruces, Kerry and Edward suggested a couple of them. They strongly felt Jake should not be with Betty, but if he had to be he would have to be in a facility that could watch them very closely so Dad would be physically and emotionally protected. Also, Jake had a bright mind and Edward knew his father needed stimulation in order to survive and get better. Edward and Kerry did their best to persuade the medical team to send him alone to a home. In fact, Edward begged to take him home to Arizona with him to find a facility for him there so he could watch over him. No. What? Only child? No say! It was going all wrong...and to make matters worse, Jake was transferred to a "memory" facility to be with his wife! Oh my God! No! But it was to be. But who could have persuaded the team of doctors..."the girls", of course!

Eldon had lost his wife about a year before Jake's "accident". He remarried. Marye was a wonderful woman and Eldon was delighted to have a new beginning. They agreed to meet with Edward and Kerry over the concerns they both had for Jake. Marye did not want to meet that nasty couple; she had heard from the girls what horrible people they were.

They stole from Jake. They needed money. They never came to visit him. Edward was always rude to his father. They were bad and she did not want to sit through a meal with them. Eldon had met Edward before, never Kerry, but he knew Jake always spoke highly of his son and his wife. What was going on here? As they ate and talked, Marye began to think she got the wrong story about this couple. What the hell was happening? It would all get settled, eventually. Unfortunately, not right away!

Edward and Kerry began to show up every weekend. They drove each time...Friday night until Sunday and during the summer they came for a few days at a time every other week. They visited at the nursing home. News of Betty's behavior was bad...she was constantly hitting Jake at night, but Jake would not admit to it. He had sores on his head, scratches on his arms. Eldon and Edward met more often, talked more often about the concern for Jake. Jake could not go back to his house again, and the home was under Eldon's care. Jake told Edward to go into the house, take his military foot locker and give it to Tommy, his great grandson. He told Edward to take what he wanted. So Eldon and Marye opened the house to Edward and he took Alice's paintings and the wood bowls that his father bought in Hawaii. Jake had a collection of coins. He told Eldon, his Power of Attorney, to send the coins to his five great grandchildren for college. They did. Marye and Eldon sweated over figuring out which coins were worth what amount and tried to disperse them as evenly as possible. They sent them to the two grandsons, Lee and Kevin, for their grandfather's legacy. Jake was satisfied. His wishes had been fulfilled so far. Also, as Marye and Eldon had gone looking for the coins, they came across two very important items that verified Jake's military career; his flight book and his book of promotions, notice of medals, and other military and Boeing documents. They immediately gave them to Jake's son. Edward had tears in his eyes, as he had never seen them before and the value to him was as great as his baseball cards had been, maybe even more so. It was sad, but what was sadder was the fact Jake was still in danger. What would happen to him? For the first time in his life, this was not a near miss. It was a direct hit!

Chapter 24 -- Exploitation

A war hero. A man that whoever met him fell under his charm. Nelson Edward Jacobs. A man who sacrificed his life and his own well being for America and for the people he loved. An honest, good man. So, how did he get himself into such a predicament at the end of his life; a broken hip, lack of control over his own legacy and destiny, and feeling unloved by his mate? It is a simple and painful truth; he was taken advantage of because he was trusting.

Babe's son in law knew his wife's mother, Betty, needed to be taken care of and there was no way he wanted to do it. Neither did his wife or her sister. Their brother had already washed his hands of her. Their mother was self centered and demanding. They felt guilty, so when she began talking about her first love, Nelson, again, someone had to do something about it. Maybe, just maybe, if Barbara's husband could connect with this Nelson man, he could "set them up." After all, the story in the family was that this Nelson guy jilted poor Betty on the door step of her Arkansas home and ran off to join the Marines. What kind of a man just leaves someone like that? Then the letters he sent. Babe's kids saw them all. All their lives. They were told to not let their father know, but they knew her real love, or addiction, was with this Nelson guy! Thank goodness for computers and the fact that Barbara and her husband were good with them. They located Nelson. Just in time. His wife of 53 years was dead;

now was the time to pounce. A phone call. Betty agreed to it, and she met him at the Houston Airport, not his sister. Jake always felt a little bad about his first lie (or maybe third) of his life. But, they were once again connected. His Babe! How romantic! Too bad Betty had not changed and too bad she had raised two very deceiving daughters, because Jake, the war hero and dedicated husband and father, did not deserve what happened to him at the age of 96!

No one really blames "Babe", not Eldon, not Edward. Betty came back into Jake's life when he needed someone. There are no promises how one leaves this world, but the best friend and the son wanted more for this great man. They tolerated Betty for Jake's sake, but they began to realize "the girls" had been taking advantage of Jake for years. Both men felt it was dangerous for Jake to be with Betty, did not think the home he was in was stimulating enough for him, and they felt their hands were tied. The girls became more out of control. Since the Chrysler van was under the name of Jake and Betty, Barbara decided she would drive it back to her home in her home state back east and keep it! That made no sense to Eldon, so he checked in with Jake. Jake looked at him in a strange way, and said, "No. That is my van." Since it became more apparent that Barbara had a key to the Las Cruces house, which was in Jake's name only, Eldon decided to take the van out of the garage, park it in his own garage for a couple days and to stop Barbara from taking it. The result was blind fury from Barbara and a threat of a law suit. Eldon told her "to go for it" because he had "no idea" where the van was. Mmmm. A man has to do what a man has to do! But then, another shoe was dropped by "the girls". One morning after Jake and Betty had breakfast, Barbara and her husband arrived at the nursing home with a document in their hands. Asking the director of the home to be the witness, handed a pen to Jake and told him he needed to sign the paper. Later it was found that Jake never read the paper but signed it because he trusted Barbara and her husband. The director signed as the witness. Unbeknown to Jake, he had just signed everything he owned over to Betty and her daughters including the van, bank accounts, and his house. The only way Eldon heard of it was Jake mentioned it in passing later that day when Eldon came in to see how Jake was doing. Dwelling deeper into what was in the document, Jake did not really know; but the director did! Eldon immediately went to the office of Jake's new lawyer, who just happened to also have been advising "the girls", and demanded to see the paper since he was the Power of Attorney. She gave him a copy. Eldon almost fainted. Jake had signed over everything to "the girls" and their mother. Eldon was furious! And that is when shit hit the fan.

Eldon felt Jake needed a custodian; someone who could actually make decisions on his behalf. Eldon got a hold of the New Mexico Adult Protection Services, an organization a lot like Child Protection Services, that takes action to help elderly adults who are suspected of being abused or exploited. Assigned to the case were Sandy and Alena, "the angels" that they later became known as in the Arizona Jacobs' and Eldon and Marye's households. APS sent in psychologists to test Jake for his mental capacity and emotional well being. They found he was highly intelligent and used that to function well enough to "fool" people into thinking he had control of his life. The physical tests followed. All indicated that Jake needed a custodian and conservator, a person assigned to manage someone's financial affairs and it would not be a relation. A Las Cruces lawyer, Jill Virgil Johnson got the case. She controlled the temporary guardianship and the finances. Sandy and Alena visited Jake and checked out the home he was in with Betty. That did not go well for the home. The director did not have the proper and legal paperwork necessary on Jake. They also found out that Jake was paying $10,000 per month for their stay. Way too much! And why wasn't Betty paying her own? Time to get the courts involved. Ms. Johnson and the judge sent out a woman well verse in interviewing family members and friends to figure out who was trustworthy. The angels did some of their own research and employed private detectives to get down to the real truth. Interestingly, the private investigation showed that Edward was financially well off with a gorgeous Scottsdale home and certainly did not need his father's money. Betty had a house that was being lived in by her daughter, Susan. That would had been okay, except Susan lied to the State of New Mexico saying she did not live there. She did. Oops for her! Jake knew nothing of the investigations. He would have had a hard time with it and he already had a lot on his plate; controlling his wife!

Edward and Kerry continued their visits to 'ole dad! They were super annoyed that he was with Betty, a dangerous situation indeed. Jake was always thrilled to see his son and to get the fresh batch of Kerry's cookies. Kerry would take Betty for a walk outside through the home's gardens so Jake and Edward could have time alone to talk. Margaret would complain after her usual sweet "Oh, this is lovely, Thank you." Then, the complaining about Jake and the food and on and on and on. Jake never complained. He asked Edward about his work and Edward asked him about his life. Jake never answered except to say, "Food is pretty good." It was like pulling teeth to get anything of substance out of him. But the woman from the court appointed by the judge got information from Jake. She learned Jake was very proud of his son and that Edward visited him often, and also, that Edward always helped him when he needed him. Jake was committed to his second wife of 53 years and he felt responsible for Betty. The only wife he said he loved was his first wife, Virginia. After several more questions, Isabella, the court appointee, had determined Jake's feelings towards everyone involved including the girls. He had said they were his wife's daughters so he felt he needed to trust them and that they were always nice to him. He knew Betty wanted to see them so he had bought their airline tickets to and from El Paso. What? Did they not pay for anything? Edward and Kerry had noticed that Betty did not pay for anything; not Costco groceries, not the commissary, not the house bills, not her clothing. Nothing! Everyone just assumed she did not have money. Then Isabella interviewed Edward and Kerry about Jake, his life with his father as a youngster, their life in Arizona. It went on and on. Then, Isabella, shook her head and said, "After interviewing you and Betty's daughters, I know who is telling the truth now. It was a pleasure to meet you. We know now what is best for your dad." After that, things began to move along better.

As APS dug deeper into expenses coming and going and where Jake's money had gone, they realized Jake paid for everything. As they got deeper into it, they found Betty actually had a higher monthly income and higher monetary worth. And, yet, she paid for nothing! Finally, it was agreed that Betty and Jake should not and could not live together anymore so Sandy and Alena moved him to a group home more accommodating to his needs; physically and mentally! The Haciendas was a group home with caregivers meeting his physical therapy needs, social needs, and helping him to emotionally cope. It felt more like home, but Jake missed Betty, or perhaps, he felt guilty he was no longer with her to take care of her. Phone calls were allowed between them and they spoke every other day. That pleased Jake and he got along as best he could knowing he could never go home to his house or live with Betty, at least for a while. There were restraining orders against the girls. Haciendas staff was to screen phone calls and not let anyone enter that was not on Jake's list of allowed visitors. The relief Eldon and Edward felt was huge! Since temporary custody was all they had for Jake, the girls tried to get it. Of course, so did Edward. But, following the legal procedures, Sandy got custody. Thank God! A court hearing occurred in February and it was brutal. Not only was it ascertained that Jake needed the custody appointed by the state, but that the girls could not be near Jake or speak to him. Betty could speak with him on the phone, but no visitations. What came out in court was astounding. There were over 25 witnesses about the abuse Jake took from Betty. How Betty scared off every care giver in town; there were no more to hire. No one wanted to get near that household. The girls argued Jake was married to their mother and he had to continue to pay $5000 a month for her. The judge said, "No. The New Mexico law says that if a spouse has money, he or she must pay her fair share." Since proof was that Betty did not even buy one thing towards their living expenses over the past nine years of marriage, she actually owed Jake money. You could hear her daughters gasping and clutching their chairs trying not to faint. The judge determined that the court hearing was to appoint a permanent custodian and conservator for Jake, the money would have to be battled out later. Since Jake had put in at least $60,000 towards Betty's care alone, the judge made a good call. At the time being, everyone who knew and loved Jake, was thankful for the ruling. Jake kept his poise as he always had done; but inside he was afraid of his future and of being without someone to love him.

The girls tried to call and see Jake before the court hearing, but afterwards they seemed to disappear into thin air. They left their mother in Las Cruces which told everyone how much they really did not care about her. It must have devastated them to pay $5000 a month out of their inheritance, but the changed will gave their mother 2/3 of Jake's estate; just as they had manipulated it! They would just have to wait it out for that would add to their inheritance since their mother did not need it! One thing they knew, if they continued their exploitation of Jake, they would find themselves in court with orders to repay what their mother did not pay in the first place. Who knew? Maybe they would even go to jail for their illegal document. The greedy girls must have thought it was best to leave quietly!

Jake was taken back to the Haciendas and Edward went back to Scottsdale determined more than ever to get custody of his father and move him to Arizona.

Chapter 25 – The Final Custody!

Jake was tired and frightened, but no one could tell. Jake at the age of 96 had lost control of where he would live, who he could see, but not what he could think. And think he did! As "the angels", Sandy and Alena said goodbye to him and helped him into his son's Audi, he knew he would never see Las Cruces again. He was okay with that! His son had received custody of him by employing a lawyer in Phoenix, going through a state training program, and receiving the permission and blessing of the Las Cruces lawyer who handled Jake's case for the State of New Mexico, Jill Virgil Johnson. Ed finally had his dad and with Kerry in the back seat, he firmly made sure his father was seat belted in and comfortable before beginning the 5 ½ hour trip to his new group home in Scottsdale, Arizona. Between "the angels" and Kerry, a very reputable home was selected within just a few miles from Edward's house. Kerry had furnished his room with new "manly" furniture, pictures on the wall of Jake's family including Space #3 and Betty. Included on the wall were Jake's favorite ball caps; the Arkansas Razorbacks, USMC Korea, USMC WWII, LSU. Scenic views of Seattle area and Hawaii were placed so he could enjoy his "favorite" locations. He had a big screen TV, a remote that was easy to use, and his clothes in the closet. Best of all, he had promise of daily visits from his loved ones and fresh cookies baked and delivered.

As they drove through the desert, the only drink or food Jake needed was a cold, icy coke from McDonalds. No problem. He sat in the front and watched the scenery go by. A torrential rainstorm hit as they traveled through Tucson, with Jake complimenting Edward about how he drove and never moved a muscle; eyes always on the road, hands on the wheel, excellent job! But, within the city of Phoenix, Jake showed the "kids" how nervous he was by asking if he could just stay on their couch for one night before going to the new group home! It made Kerry cry, but she knew it wasn't possible. Jake was at the point that he needed people around him who knew how to care for him; move him to stand and walk with his walker, help him to the toilet and not let him fall. It scared Edward and Kerry to even think about getting him out of the car...what if they broke him? They promised to stay with him until he felt comfortable and that they would be there every day to see him.

Thank God for the excellent people that greeted the Jacobs' family at the home. As they assisted Jake inside to his room, he sat in the chair, looked out of the window next to him, and gave a sigh of relief. He admitted to himself it felt good and he would be fine. He knew he had to be fine and, once again, he knew he had to acclimate. The real emotional problem he had was that just that morning of July 15, 2014, he had spoken to Betty expecting to tell her he was going on a visit to Arizona. Before he could utter a word, she blurted out that her daughter, Susan, was there to take her back to Houston, forever. What? Where did that come from? Jake was shocked. He felt Susan had pulled his wife from him and once again felt, deserted. For weeks Jake worried about Betty. He wanted to call her. The Angels back in Las Cruces tried to find her and get a phone number so he could call, but no one seemed to know where she was. Eldon tried. Kerry and Edward tried. Dead end. Finally, after stressing every day about if Betty was okay, Sandy found out some news. She had been placed in a Houston nursing home and she was being taken care of under the "watchful" eye of her daughters. He felt better but he never fully recovered from "the girls" just taking her like that! By the time Edward had been able to get custody, Jake knew how the girls were. He never complained about them. He never talked bad about them. But he knew. He said nothing, but Edward and Eldon could see his hurt and how exhausted he had become. They knew this would be his final earthly move. His son planned to make it a good one for him!

Every day Edward would go to the home and visit his father. Most days Kerry went with him or went after school to visit alone with him. Jake would light up when his only child walked in. He would smile his little grin, and ask what he could get them. Nothing, of course. He was delighted to hear about his oldest great grandson, Chris, going to Embry Riddle Aeronautical University in Prescott, Arizona and every day used the ERAU drink container that held his raspberry-cranberry juice. The university he knew quite well, in fact, it brought back memories for himself, as he had once studied at ERAU in Florida during his flight training many years before.

Jake's true friend, Eldon, arrived in Arizona to visit within a month of his move. Marye gave Jake his haircut which Jake had missed since leaving Las Cruces. He would only let Marye cut his very thinning hair line. It was a somber but joyous get together. Sadly and unbeknown at the time, it was the last time Eldon would see his best friend.

His caregivers were concerned about his eating; he did not eat much. But when Todd, Kerry's youngest son, cooked chili for him, he wolfed it down. He enjoyed talking to Todd. He described him as a well mannered young man with a great smile and he named him "Chili Boy". He even talked to him a little about the action he saw during WWII and his bombing of the Japanese. He told Todd, "I bombed the hell out of 'em. They didn't like it much, but neither did I." Wow. Jake expressed his feelings.

Christy visited her grandfather several times while in Scottsdale, telling him fun stories about her writing adventures in Hollywood. And Jake marveled at her book she had written. He had some experience in writing, so he respected what a gift being able to put words down on paper could be. Kevin and his family came over from California to see Jake. What a thrill that was for Jake. Becca and Bella spent the time drawing posters for the walls of Jake's room, while Mandy, Kevin, Edward and Kerry visited with Jake. He grinned and chuckled. And when the posters were hung up in his room, he showed them off to everyone who entered his room. He felt loved. He felt wanted. He was.

Edward was with his father every time a doctor or nurse came in to check on him. He was involved in every medical decision. He helped the care givers with ideas on how to help his father and assisted them as much as he could, but the most important thing was being with his father under their rules; just father and son with no interferences. What an amazing time it was for both of them. They shared memories, good and bad. They shared times in their lives they wanted the other one to know. They even shared, with a grin, how their lives were similar in a few ways; three marriages, leaving home in a hurried way, desertion from their biological mother, vanilla ice cream. They talked and talked. Every day. And everyday Edward would bring him a gourmet chocolate. One was okay at first but within a couple weeks Edward had to give him two and leave him one for later. He did love his chocolate. Kerry stopped making cookies, because Jake never ate them. He wanted chili, chocolate, or onion rings from Burger King. Why not?

Kerry would rub Jake's head with Lubriderm lotion every time she went to see him. He almost liked that as much as the chocolate his son brought him. She would massage his head, and he just gave a little groan. It felt good. He felt loved. She would also bring him onion rings. He loved his onion rings, so they would sit and eat them and talk about the Pacific Northwest. Since Kerry was born and raised there, they had a grand ole time remembering the positives of that part of the United States including razor clam digging. But, even the head rubs, onion rings, chocolate and chili could not make Jake live forever. Edward hoped he had his father for at least a year, but it was not to be. The cancer had returned and his father was becoming weaker.

Lee and his wife, Vera, and their two children Sophie and Tommy arrived in the second week of November. Delighted to meet his two great grandchildren, Jake became more alert than he had been in a while. Tommy, age 6, looked like Edward when he was little, so Jake was totally fascinated with him. He was almost startled to see him; he felt he had been transformed back into time. He had to shake his head to clear it and realize it was his great grandchild standing before him, not his son. As Jake brought Tommy and Sophie, closer to him, he quietly said to them. "Do you know how old I am? 96. That is good news for the two of you." Hee-hee! He chorkled. The two children played the piano and sang for Jake, with the rest of the residents enjoying it too. Jake tired easily so everyone left him with hugs and kisses.

Nelson Edward Jacobs had his last head rub, chocolate, and hugs on November 18, 2014. He died with Edward and Kerry next to him. He died with dignity. He did not die alone. He was with people who loved him dearly.

With 212 university hours under his belt, medals on his uniform, America safe, one son, three grandchildren and five great grandchildren surviving him, Jake was buried at Ft. Bliss National Cemetery on February 15, 2015 next to Alice. As he had wished. The Angels, Kevin's mother in law, his grandchildren, Eldon, Marye, Kerry and Edward said goodbye at the gravesite after he was given the Military Funeral Honors Ceremony with taps played and a 21 gun salute. May he rest in peace. Jake deserves it.

RESOURCES

Useers.idworld.net. Idworld.net, 16 July 2001. Web. 18 July 2016.

"4th Marines Small Unit Histories."

"4th Marine Regiment (United States)." Military Wiki. N.p., n.d. Web. 19 Aug. 2016.

<http://military.wikia.com/wiki/4th_Marine_Regiment_(United_States)>.

"25th Infantry Division (United States)." Wikipedia. Wikimedia Foundation, n.d. Web. 19 June 2015.

<https://en.wikipedia.org/wiki/25th_Infantry_Division_%28United_States%29>.

"Arms Industry." Wikipedia, the Free Encyclopedia. N.p., n.d. Web. 29 July 2016.

<http://en.metapedia.org/wiki/Arms_industry>.

Battle of Okinawa-World War II. Web. 11 June 2016. <History.com>.

"The Boeing Company Facts, Information, Pictures." *Encyclopedia. Encyclopedia.com, n.d. Web. 2 Aug. 2016.*

<www.encyclopedia/com/topic/The_Boeing_Company.aspx>.

Cat, Ginny and Steve, and Major Jarhead. "USMC-342-VMSB-245."*Geocaching.com. N.p., n.d. Web. 27 June 2016.*

"China Marines." *Chinamarines.com. N.p., n.d. Web. 19 June 2015.*

<www.chinamarines.com/ver3/shan/htm>.

"China Marines | HistoryNet." *HistoryNet. N.p., 12 June 2006. Web. 19 June 2015.*

<http://www.historynet.com/china-marines.htm>.

"A Chronology of Selected Events Associated with Marine Corps Activities in China." *The China Marines Chronology.*

N.p., 22 Nov. 2010. Web. 19 June 2016. <http://chinamarine.org/Chronology.aspx>.

"COLONEL JOHN H. GLENN, JR, PROMINENT UNITED STATES MARINES."COLONEL JOHN H. GLENN, JR,

    PROMINENT UNITED STATES MARINES. N.p., n.d. Web. 27 June 2016. <http://www.usmarinesbirthplace.com/GLENN.html>.

"Crossing." The China Marines. N.p., 22 Nov. 2010. Web. 19 June 2016. <http://chinamarine.org/Crossing.aspx>.

"Curtiss SB2C Helldiver." – Wikipedia. N.p., n.d. Web. 13 July 2015.

"Curtiss SB2C Helldiver - Development and Operational History, Performance Specifications and Picture

    Gallery." Curtiss SB2C Helldiver. N.p., n.d. Web. 8 Aug. 2015.

"Dive Bomber." - Wikipedia. N.p., n.d. Web. 19 July 2015.

"Douglas SBD Dauntless." Militaryfactory.com. Militaryfactory.com, n.d. Web. 4 Aug. 2015.

<www.militaryfactory.com/aircraft/detail.asp?aircraft_id=297>

"Feature The China Marines." PBS. PBS, n.d. Web. 19 June 2015.

<http://www.pbs.org/opb/historydetectives/feature/the-china-marines/>.

"Fort Lawton Air Force Station." Wikipedia. Wikimedia Foundation, n.d. Web. 29 July 2016.

<https://en.wikipedia.org/wiki/Fort_Lawton_Air_Force_Station>.

Frame, Rudy R., Ssgt. "MCA&F." Okinawa: The Final Great Battle of World War II. N.p., Nov. 2012. Web. 11 June

2016. <https://www.mca-marines.org/gazette/2012/11/okinawa-final-great-battle-world-war-ii>.

"Google." Google. N.p., n.d. Web. 29 July 2016.

    <http://www.google.com/search?z=phantom%2Blakebellevue&riz=1C2LDJZ_enUS499US524&biw=1920&bh=inmas&ved=OahUKEw17-77kv>.

"Hollywood Brown Derby Home Page." Hollywood Brown Derby Home Page. N.p., n.d. Web. 29 June 2016.

<http://www.originalhollywoodbrownderby.com/>.

"HyperWar: USMC Operations in WWII: Vol IV--Western Pacific Operations [Chapter IV-2]." HyperWar: USMC

Operations in WWII: Vol IV--Western Pacific Operations [Chapter IV-2]. N.p., n.d. Web. 11 June 2016. <http://www.ibiblio.org/hyperwar/USMC/IV/USMC-IV-IV-2.html>.

"Lineage Of The Fourth Marine Regiment." Lineage Of The Fourth Marine Regiment. N.p., 5 Dec. 2010. Web. 19

"Jaluit." The Pacific War Online Encyclopedia:. N.p., n.d. Web. 11 June 2016.

<http://www.pwencycl.kgbudge.com/J/a/Jaluit.htm>. June 2016. <http://1stbn4thmarines.net/history-of-14.html>.

"MCA&F." Okinawa: The Final Great Battle of World War II. N.p., n.d. Web. 11 June 2016.

<https://www.mcamarines.org/gazette/2012/11/okinawa-final-great-battle-world-war-ii>.

"Marine Corps Air Station El Toro." Marine Corps Air Station El Toro. Historynet, n.d. Web. 15 July 2016.

<history.net.com/curtiss-sb2c-heldiver-the-last-dive-bomber.htm>.

"News - HeraldNet.com - Everett and Snohomish County, Washington."HeraldNet.com. N.p., n.d. Web. 29 July 2016.

<http://www.heraldnet.com/article/20120325/BLOG48/703259916/-1/NEWS>.

"Hurricane Dot |." Extremeplanet.com. N.p., n.d. Web. 26 July 2016. <https://extremeplanet.me/tag/hurricane-dot/>.

"Military Intelligence." Wikipedia. Wikimedia Foundation, n.d. Web. 26 July 2016.

<https://en.wikipedia.org/wiki/Military_intelligence>.

National Weather Service." The 1959 Central Pacific Tropical Cyclone Season. National Weather Service, n.d. Web.

26 July 2016. <http://www.prh.noaa.gov/cphc/summaries/1959.php>.

"Navy Flier Crashes, Cheats Death 10,000 Times from Machine Gun Fire."Camp Callan [San Diego, California] 2

Dec. 1943, 36th ed.: n. pag. Web. 04 Dec. 2014.

"Nelson Jacobs." United States Census. United States Census, n.d. Web. 27 July 2015.

<https://familysearch.org/ark:/61903/1:1:XM2B-FRL>.

"Nelson Edward Jacobs." *Nelson Edward Jacobs*. Memphis, TN Commercial Appeal, Sept. *1999*. Web. 18 Aug. *2000*. <http://www.xphomestation.com/njacobs.html>.

Niderost, Eric. "Military History Online - China Marines: The Lost Leathernecks." *Military History Online - China Marines: The Lost Leathernecks*. N.p., n.d. Web. *19 June 2016*.

"Old China." *The China Marines*. N.p., *22 Nov. 2010*. Web. *19 June 2016*.

<http://chinamarine.org/OldChina.aspx>.

Oshiro, Coach Les. "Schofield Sharks Swim Club (SSSC)." Editorial. n.d.: n. pag. Web. *26 July 2016*

<http://www.hawaiiswim.org/learn/01schofield.html>.

"Peking." *The China Marines*. N.p., *22 Nov. 2010*. Web. *19 June 2016*.

<http://chinamarine.org/Peking.aspx>.

"Pacific Wrecks." - Mili Atoll (Mille). N.p., n.d. Web. 27 June 2016.

<http://www.pacificwrecks.com/provinces/marshall_mili.html>.

Rent Review Commission." The Hemet News [Hemet] 11 Jan. 1991: n. pag. Web.

"Reserve Officers' Training Corps." Wikipedia, the Free Encyclopedia. N.p., n.d. Web. 31 July 2016.

<https://en.wifipedia.org/wiki/Reserve_Officers%17_Training_Corps>.

Roberts, Nolle T., SGT. "MCA&F." Chesty Puller. N.p., June 1948. Web. 19 June 2015.

<http://www.mca-marines.org/leatherneck/chesty-puller>.

"Schofield Barracks." Wikipedia, the Free Encyclopedia. N.p., n.d. Web. 26 July 2016.

<https%3A%2F%2Fen.wikipedia.org%2Fwiki%2FSchofield_Barracks>.

"Service Management Project Manager Job Description at Boeing." Service Management Project Manager Job

Description at Boeing. N.p., n.d. Web. 29 July 2016.

<https://jobs.boeing.com/job/milton-keynes/service-management-project-manager/185/2175825>.

"Shangai." N.p., 22 Nov. 2010. Web. 16 June 2016.

<http://chinamarine.org/Shanghai/ShanghaiToday.aspx>.

Shettle, M. L., Jr. "Historic California Posts: Marine Corps Air Station, El Toro."Historic California Posts: Marine Corps Air Station, El Toro. N.p., n.d. Web. 14 June 2016.

<http://www.militarymuseum.org/MCASEToro.html>.

"The Story: Friends Really Can Drop out of the Sky." Barnstorming. N.p., n.d. Web. 31 July 2015.

<http://www.barnstormingmovie.com/film.htm>.

Tientsin Today." The China Marines Tientsin. N.p., 22 Nov. 2010. Web. 19 June 2016.

<http://chinamarine.org/Tientsin/TientsinToday.aspx>.

Transportation.army.mil. N.p., n.d. Web. 1 Aug. 2016.

<www.transportation.army.mil/museum/transportation%20museum/korearail>.

U. S. Army War College; "Campaign Planning Handbook." *Department of Military Strategy, Planning, and Operations AY 08 (2008)*: Vii. Web. 17 July 2016.

"U.S. Policy Changed At End of 1937." *Mac.com*. N.p., n.d. Web. 19 June 2016.

"USMC Slogans." *USMC Slogans*. N.p., n.d. Web. 7 July 2016.

<http://www.usmcpress.com/heritage/usmc_slogans.htm>.

"The United States Army | Fort Benning." *The United States Army | Fort Benning*. N.p., n.d. Web. 17 July 2016.

<http://www.benning.army.mil/mcoe/usmc/mccc.html>.

"Ulithi Atoll." – *Wikipedia*. N.p., n.d. Web. 29 June 2016.

<https://sv.wikipedia.org/wiki/Ulithi_Atoll>.

Wahiawa, HI." *DoDHN.com*. City of Wahiawa, HI, n.d. Web. 26 July 2016.

NEAR MISSES

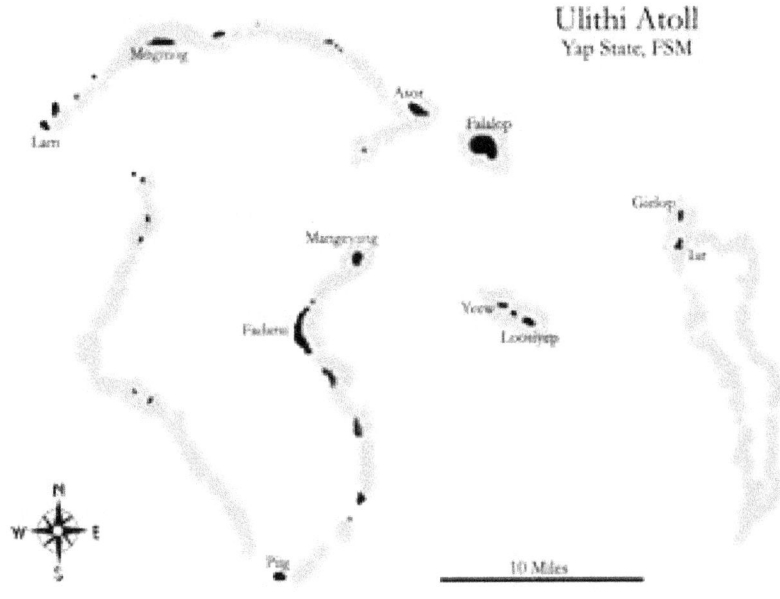

NEAR MISSES

www.ingramcontent.com/pod-product-compliance
Lightning Source LLC
Chambersburg PA
CBHW042112120526
44592CB00042B/2699